Sometimes It's Heaven

Also by Judy Collins

Cravings: How I Conquered Food
Sweet Judy Blue Eyes: My Life in Music
Over the Rainbow
The Seven T's: Finding Hope and Healing in the Wake of Tragedy
Morning, Noon, and Night: Living the Creative Life
Sanity and Grace: A Journey of Suicide, Survival, and Strength
Singing Lessons: A Memoir of Love, Loss, Hope, and Healing
Shameless
Voices (CD including songbook and memoir)
My Father
Trust Your Heart: An Autobiography

Sometimes It's Heaven

Poems of Love, Loss, and Redemption

Judy Collins

Andrews McMeel
PUBLISHING®

Dedication
To my ancestors who made the
paths on which I travel
The ones who dreamed the dreams that I
would live

Prologue

Poetry is a resource for living on the planet. The art we practice comes for us—while we are having our coffee in the morning, while we are meeting someone we haven't seen in years and share a smile and share the tears. There are always tears. There are always smiles. There are always streets—where you meet the past and the future.

The pages of my life are turning—over and over I see the visions that have haunted my dreams. I'm a traveler in the world, and destiny has taken me millions of miles—in airplanes and cars and trains as the landscapes fly and the mind takes its turn over mountains and along the sides of rivers and plains, along long-forgotten dreams that overtake the miles and years. The moment at hand is all that counts—and I have learned that living today is what I need to do—loving today, dreaming today, and making what poem I can in the moment. I take the light with whatever is haunting me—whatever is delighting me—whoever's faces—the lovers, my family, the people who have shaped my destiny. My journeys to the past and my memories of people and places form a way to turn the looking glass outward from my own reflection and bring to life moments that I sometimes think I've forgotten. And I love to fly! My heart lifts when I take off in a plane—the landscapes of Arizona or Colorado or Australia bring me to my senses, to my memories. And music unearths these memories for me. One of the reasons I sing is so that I can remember and my audiences can remember deeply hidden memories, the ones that yearn to be looked at more closely. Creativity helps us believe in our own survival, past fear or dreams or unknown visions, or to float among the dust of the heavens and hope to hear that heavenly choir. Today we stand and breathe our share of breath, our share of pain—while the unbearable may happen, there is unbelievable joy that is possible and that is part of living. I hope that reading these poems will encourage you to see the joy as well as overcome the trouble. I hope you will pick up the pen beside your bed, the device that tells you where to go and what to do—and write your own poetry.

Poetry is the blessed doorway.

I.   The Girl That I Was

The girl that I was
had the courage to live fast and wild
She tore into life with nerve
and was never defiled
She shouted her love
and her anger like she was possessed
Took chances and changes
They were always part of her quest
As though the chances
she took had never had penalty
she always had secret lovers
hidden obsessively
The girl that I was had no fears
about life or of death
She was willing to run in the wind
and exhaust her last breath
Her eyes saw no shadows
Her heart wasn't broken with grief
Her meandering glance saw no menace
Her anger was brief
That girl—when I need her
if only—if it could be now
I would bring her to stand with me
then I would give her a bow
She was the beginning of everything
She was the best
I try to live up to her
She was the girl from the West

2.   O'Keeffe

Looking at O'Keeffe
I see white bones in a blue sky
On the red, rocky ridge below the clouds
As the heavens bellow
Wind through the hollows
Under the shelter of shadows
Dreams like raw whiskey spilled in the sand
You saw flowers the way you saw fear
The way you saw dreams
Rivers of crimson soaked in tangerine
The stamens of the petals, the colors of orchids
The spotted violet on the bright green ground
The vagina flaring in the bosom of the rose
The curl of the bone in the face of the steer
The brush in your thin, tanned hands
Your long legs running
From Stieglitz, from the galleries
From the power and those who would crush you
Grabbing the brush from your hand
Sapping the cobalt from the tube
To cut you like a bloom of purple from the
Blazing violet.
Forty days, forty nights and you were gone
Into the dust of summer
And the clear skies of winter
Into the canyons of Santa Fe
From the skyscrapers of New York City
To the desert where you painted yourself
     Into a corner of the world
     Where almost no one could chase you
     You settled the score.
          You wanted more.
          I want more.

3.   Clark

He had red hair and blue eyes
He was pulled out of me with forceps
on January 8, 1959
after twenty-eight hours of labor
He weighed nine pounds and two ounces
I gave birth in Boulder where we lived and my husband Peter was
getting his Master's degree—
Clark was born in a Jehovah's Witness hospital in the shadow of
the Flatirons
They served no coffee and no meat
                        I ate mushroom loaf and drank tea
and nursed this boy
We named him Clark
He laughed early and smiled often
                        He was totally bright and shiny and
smart as a whip
He sang early and loved his mother's singing and loved his mother
He grew up tall like his dad
I started singing for money to support my son and my husband (whose
name I used for seven weeks that I remember)
I had a pack for Clark and we tooled around Boulder, Colorado
                        shopping and doing the laundry
        while Pete was in school
I sang at night and Peter did his homework
                        and took care of Clark
                        It was a good life
When I got my first gig at Michael's Pub
I was making a hundred dollars a week
and we moved from Mrs. Tingly's
basement apartment
to a little log cabin on a river in Boulder
Drinking started slow and increased fast
I made batches of home brew à la
John Clark, our Long's Peak ranger friend

Some of the bottles always
blew up in the closet
What a mess
I picked Clark up and swept the glass off the floor
and went to work
We had a husky named Smokey
and by the time I left for my big career
I was divorced from my
starter husband and fighting
to have custody of my
beautiful boy
which eventually I won
We lived happily ever after
until his death by his own hand in 1992
He died as had his paternal grandfather,
Gary Taylor—sometime in 1948—
in a car in a garage
with the motor running
      Rest In Peace, my beautiful boy

4. The Angel

The angel comes through the door
The one that you've seen before
She's shining in the light
So beautiful, so bright
In a graceful shaft she hovers
While you stayed beneath the covers
But today is different
You'd hoped and prayed that you would die
No more fight in the mind
No defense of any kind
This day is no different at all
But you answer the angel's call
Why today does she stay in sight?
Why the sudden light?
When all of these days you've fought her
No matter how much you sought her
You weren't going to give in easy
But today your arms reach freely
And suddenly you're in the light
You know it will be all right
You turn to the angel's face
Fall into her arms with grace
At once you know you're safe
No longer the lonely waif
Wandering through your day
Your life in disarray
Joy comes into view
It's all so strange and new
The joy that's coming through to you

5. A River of Stars

The stars fell out of the black sky
An owl watched in the trees
I saw my shadow dancing
Moving with grace and ease
Running through the willows
Onto the hills of home
I saw the old illusions
Dying and I was alone
I heard the call of the eagle
I saw his wings spread wide
The air was bright with thunder
Over the countryside
Now, I said, fly higher
Over the peaks and hills
Take me to the summit
Wherever the goddess wills
The sun breathed fire and slaughter
The moon over land
Forever happened quickly
I took time in my hand
All alone in the summer
The wind had gone and died
I turned to my future
The past was tall and wide
You stood there smiling sweetly
As lovely as sin
You said, now all is over
It's time we can begin

6   In the Ruins of Your Beauty
For MT

In the ruins
    of your beauty
    I can see beyond the years
        to the bridge where we were standing
    at the start of all those tears
When your body was a signal
    to the lives we both would lead
There together in the hurricane
    the willows and the weeds
Fifty years ago today
    my old memories hold the key
As you chased the clouds away
    I saw what you could see
But even as we kissed beyond
    the pounding of the waves
I knew we'd ride the years
    and then regret we'd been so brave
To know the secrets, know the sins
    that lead us to today
With courage we began to make
    the journey—walk and pray
We had a perfect start
    but our romance could not stand
I was lingering; the heart stared back
    from sea and wind and land
And now your look reminds me
    what I left there in my youth
Out of reach and out of vision
    until now I see the truth
That we were meant to live
    far from that timeless beauty
Foraging life among the broken rules
    the loss of duty

The power still is haunting
        in your long-remembered face
The day was beaten gold
        as I gathered in your grace
The old familiar tugging
        keen and true and free and wild
Now I remembered everything
Your voice was kind and mild
        Your face still burns my heart
          your passion not gone yet
And I know that you still love me
        and I know I won't forget
          beyond our ruins

7.   Fern Lake

We had no money that summer
just a woodstove that needed feeding
The little chess game sat on the table in the morning sun
He won every game, and after at last I shouted
"Checkmate!"
We never played again
A red marten came down by the lake each morning
his fur shining as he drank from the icy mountain water
Peter strolled up the trail to make sure the feed from the
spring was bringing our water down
I finished baking bread and pies on that woodstove
slicing Spam and throwing peanut butter and jelly onto
homemade bread-roll sandwiches
We fed them to the hikers who made it up to our lodge
Fern Lake Lodge had opened in 1916, and forty-two years later
here we were
The mountains about us were staggeringly beautiful and
evidently had always been there
Every week a pack mule hauled supplies
up from Grand Lake and Estes Park
with a handsome cowboy wearing chaps
a bottle of bourbon in his
leather-gloved hands
We had no electricity
But there was a telephone on which I called my mother
once a weekend—Daddy on the extension line
The rugged cabins were decades old
And the travelers who hiked the mountain were brave
It was nine and a half miles from one end
at Grand Lake Lodge to the
other end in the national park near the rangers' station
(Gone now, my brother Mike
told me recently, in the fire that
ripped through Rocky Mountain National Park last summer)
In the middle of that hike, it was
    eleven thousand feet through a fern-laden meadow

Spring water ran through the pipes
that came down from the mountain
It surged into the radiator that was
strapped on the back of the fireplace
and we had hot water for showers
The water poured out of upside-down
buckets just outside the back door
where Peter split the wood for the fireplace
After lunch was served
I would sit on the porch
playing the guitar and singing
"This Land Is Your Land" and "The Lavender Cowboy"
and "Streets of Laredo"
We made love in that rickety bed
by the lake in a little cabin a half-century old
Now I am thirty years over a half-century old
But the light from the pine trees
in the air of the Rocky Mountains
Paradise still makes my heart leap

8 Hockney in the Mountains

It was midnight and the party was over
Our host was tall and rugged,
a Colorado man, senior president of the foundation
David Hockney and I were honorary guests at the party
brought in to talk and raise money for someone or something we both
believed in
We were staying at
a fancy upscale condo
near the Aspen Alps
I was pretty drunk, and David
and I went out on the pine balcony to smell the woodsmoke and take
in the sharp, crisp mountain air
The summer night was cold and we were giddy
Standing there looking out at Ajax when a heart-stopping, blood-
curdling scream split the air and struck us, like knives to the heart
I said someone is having glorious sex
David said someone is being murdered
We debated for a while and then had another drink in the resuming
quiet of the mountain air
I stumbled back into the room
Our host called the man at the front desk
who said there was nothing they could do about noise in the
mountains;
everybody screams sometimes
The air was still again, as though blood had poured out of a wound
and cauterized in the freezing air
David went back to his room
I passed out and woke to the morning paper
The scream we had heard
was that of a famous skier who had been stabbed to death by his
jealous lover
in their little cabin
on the next mountainside
So hard to separate the screams of pleasure
from the screams of death

9.   Odessa

Inside the wars that block the light
I see beyond the deepest night
No birds are singing songs at dawn
and all the dreams of joy are gone
I was there in '65
singing among the apple trees
In my twenties, young and free
my blessings came in twos and threes
Odessa's port was busy then
with sailing ships and gentlemen
Their uniforms were bright and fine
as glorious as summer wine
You could not see them red with blood
upon the tree, upon the bud
or turned to shreds
deep in the flood of war

10. Like a Star

So long I did not see, see it as a gift
The trouble and the struggle and the light
The dancing that's required and the easy stuff
The cleaning and the trashing and the flight

The setting up the tables and the washing up the pans
The hollering, the bickering, the peace
I did not see it all for what it was for all those years
The music of survival and release

The holy days in pretty clothes, the singleness of purpose
The course of time through little acts of kindness
The waiting for the moment I could run like hell away
The joy I felt, and then there was the blindness

I saw it as a burden much more often than a dance
I felt that it was personal and cruel
That I had been selected from the crowd to pay the price
Now I know how long I was a fool

So now the dance is precious and the silver in the sky
Makes rain the blessing of a day
To live through trouble, something I can cling to like a prayer
And realize I'm here and I will stay

Surrounded by my weakness, my intolerance and greed
My imperfection, too human by far
And I can see the learning and the falling from the tree
The dance that keeps me rising like a star

I'm surrounded by my weakness, my intolerance and greed
My imperfection, too human by far
And I can see the learning and the falling from the tree
The dance that keeps me rising—
Rising like a star,
Like a star

11.   Agatha Christie '21

Agatha Christie
In the dark of the night
Flying from Oslo
With all my might
Comfy as an English
Cup of tea
Reading tonight will set me free
Free to drift in and out of sleep
Free to slumber, free to leap
Out of the window, above the blue sea
The whales are swimming just for me
I'm cozy in comfort
I'm leaning back
As the light dies away
The sky pitch-black
She's amazing and crisp
She's clever and clean
She's thoughtful and funny, is Agatha
Queen
She's Poirot and Miss Marple behind
She's totally free to go out of her mind
I'm reading her books like a lesson in crime
A lesson in language
A lesson in time
The reader, Hugh Fraser
Who talks me to sleep
He's read every book
Awake and asleep
I doze off
Restless to get back to all that English trifle
The sound of old intelligence

12. Thomas Merton

Put your wings in your pocket and fly like a hawk
Streaming through the morning sky
From the monastery in Louisville
Till you land in old Shanghai
Decide if you can live through the night
So you will have another day
To send your light down through the clouds
And go on, come what may
The nine fields of your universe
The touch and go—the flight
Compassion in the enterprise
Until you land at night
Easily into the peace
You'll find compassion's way
Until the flying is finally done
And at last, you can pray
When dawn comes bright upon the earth you'll
Stand under those wings
Breathing deeply of the air
You'll find that all earth sings
Ringing with the morning bells
Rising with
The sun
You will know beyond all doubt
The work has just begun

13. Delacroix

We went to see the Delacroix
The lions and the tigers
Ladies with their jewels and
Their skin as white as cream
We saw the bright cerulean
The turbans of Moroccans
Deep-ruby velvet bodices and
The horses
God, the horses!
Every one magnificent
Every one Arabian
Men dreaming through the water

With the boat full now of waving Arms
Ribboned with veins that stand stretched
On the canvas where the ocean hovers above
Their floundering boat
Redolent with white foam and
Oars beset with water roiled
Where always they will wait
Through another hundred years or so
To see how far the water falls
And if they are bound for
Drowning or for life

14.   Painting the Abyss
For Mark Rothko

I like the guy in the black hat
leaning over from his narrow waist
in front of the Rothko
the red of the painting
the white
the border between
fuzzy, a line
blue eyes
wandering the colors—
wandering me
on their way to the next—
an orange and black painting
and bending again
celebrating the edge
edging toward me
a place beyond abstraction
the artist as underdog
the audience as overdog
Rothko taking his life in his studio
slitting his wrists
it has to be beautiful
even in death

15.   Poetry

I have read my poem today
Rumi again
Afterward I seek roses in the ocean
I read Sylvia the day before
And sought knives in the linoleum
Poe funnels nightmares and blood dripping into pools
Whitman shouts America
Wallace Stevens sings of blackbirds and insurance
Frost gazes at the snow-covered trees I see among the summer leaves
Stephen Crane bends my heart in two with mustard gas
James Baldwin and I want to march and rage
Gertrude puts melodies to blank space
That otherwise is a garden of words
Perhaps tomorrow I will
Read Keats, and seek mist in the
Mums, silver in the waterfalls
Rivers in the rhinestones
Perhaps I'll turn to Woody Guthrie
For the melody

16,   Dark Night

Headlights sparkle in the gleaming drops
Windshield wipers rolling silver glass
We can't go as fast as I would like
One way up the mountain on the pass

Pine trees shedding drops of opal pearls
On the highway, rivers in a hurry
Getting to the heart of every question
Rain will do that—make you take your time

Make you think of all you thought was true
Make you wonder what you're going to do
When the sun comes out and things seem new
When you see the sky up there is blue

But for now the rain will take its time
Slow the running motors of my mind
Take a detour to some town in flood
Find a place to stop and watch the void

Let the rising waters heal my heart
Where the green has wilted in the heat
Bring me back to life and find my smile
Bring me home to love so young and wild
On a rainy night

17.   Wedding Song for Louis

The night before our wedding, I dreamed of falling stars
And all the souls that I have loved came bending to my window
A galaxy of wishes as far as I could see
I thanked the gods and goddesses for bringing you to me

You are a gift to me, freely given out of heaven
Nothing I did before could have earned your love
Somewhere a prayer was heard, someone must have seen me kneeling
And you were there for me, my own true love

I was a wandering soul when you found me in the darkness
Chasing the shadow ghosts through the distant past
I saw you wore no mask and your armor was of moonlight
When I embraced your love I was free at last

And it's time to celebrate our wedding
After all these many years
To celebrate our lives together
I'll marry you for love
I'll marry you for laughter
I'll marry you ever after

Troubadours sing of love and they speak of consolation
Cupid and Venus smile when the arrow flies
There is the pain of love when a wounded heart is broken
There is the peace that comes when it's really love

It's time to celebrate our wedding
After all these many years
To celebrate our time together
I'll marry you for love
I'll marry you for laughter
I'll marry you ever after

The night before I met you, I dreamed that I was lost
And all the demons I had known came bending to my window
The moon dissolved in tears; the stars were fire burning
But when I fell in love with you, my heartache turned to yearning

Once more the comet flies after eighteen thousand springtimes
Over our ancient vows like a shining pearl
Sorrow may come again, but the joy will keep returning
Love can do anything; love can change the world

It's time to celebrate our wedding
After all these many years
To celebrate our lives together
I'll marry you for love
I'll marry you for laughter
I'll marry you ever after

18.   An Hour from Boston

I'm an hour from Boston, I'm on the right train
I'm going to see an old lover again
He's back in the hospital, not doing well
There was a time he could just go to hell

But that was the past tense, when love was the thing
It drove us all crazy, it made us all sing
Me on the Commons and him on the wharf
He knew that I loved him, but love would soon morph

Into something different, a kind of a dream
Where people you once loved are not what they seemed
But better than most people you came to know
Over the long road one just has to hoe

So now I'm in Boston, I'll just catch the bus
I'll grab myself something for lunch with no fuss
Enough of those dinners, an arm and a leg
He'd say, so we would usually have to go Dutch

Even that was too much, the Durgen Park steak
The walks in museums, the lunch by the lake
We should have been living together in sin
Instead we just waited for life to begin

So now we've been friends for four decades or more
I answer his emails and go to the store
I buy him his paper and get his supplies
We talk about old times, and often he lies

Though I know the truth, I won't say so aloud
Two is just company, three is a crowd
I never thought we'd be laughing at us
Back in the day, there was just too much fuss

My husband approves, he's a soft-hearted guy
He knows this is just an old friend, I won't fly
And if it were him I would do just the same
Life is a mystery, love is a game

19.   Until Today

I think it's all clear
and then when I hear
the sound of your voice
through the noise
I thought I was brave
and then I would grieve
I shudder with fear
I felt you were here
I thought I was free
but then I could see
I was still alone
afraid to the bone
still with my pride
along for the ride
when we had it all
before the great fall
How could you leave
and leave me to grieve
the words
the pain
until today

20.   Traveler

I met a weary traveler
Hard by the river's swell
His voice was like the sound of rain
His singing like a bell
Dark and sweet or high and clear
Familiar as a smile
We walked along the riverbank
And talked for most a mile
He told me he had lost his way
And nearly lost his life
He'd gambled everything away
His fortune and his wife
She'd run off with a sailor
Bound for glory and for shame
He'd found another way to live
Unbounded and unblamed
And now he made his dreams his life
And lived by these alone
He had the soul of princes
He had the look of bone
Sad in eye and sweet in voice
He spoke to me in rhymes
He told me he would wait for me
Out where the trellis climbs
But when I came to rendezvous
He'd gone, as fast as smoke
Rises from the fireplace
As though we never spoke
I wish him speedy journeys
To wherever he is bound
He touched me with a simple grace
The lost beneath the found
So walking on I wish him well
He had the sweetest voice
I would have followed him so far
But did not have the choice

21.   Prayers

For Billy Collins

The glare of the ice on the road
Looking back at the ranch in the snow
Where the billy goat stands in the wind
Searching for my return
My face over the fence
Nodding hello
Nodding goodbye
Sorrow in his eyes as I lie awake
In the Gooding Hotel
The Shangri-La in Cincinnati, Ohio
Staring down the roads that lead to everywhere
To singing in the dark
Where there are no billy goats
And no fences
And no glare of ice on the road

22.   Murmuration
For A

I spied a murmuration in the sky
The birds were shifting, floating
In the air
Like smoke the wind blew feathered
Bodies flying
A dream of centuries beyond repair
Their silence as invisible as spirit
Painting their own world with
Tiny hearts
Gentle warriors in clouds uplifting
Pure as ancient fire
Primal singing
Before the ruined planet can defy them
A sight like whirling, wheeling all around
Above, within, they take our breath away
Without a sound

23.   Before I Die

I wonder when I die
what they will say
Will they remember
I was mostly happy
Will they see through
the diamonds to the dirt
Will they see
what made me curse
what made me hurt
Today someone else has died
Someone I knew but
not so well
It's always happening
It's hard to just keep up
so I wonder if they'll
see my soul as
perfect or imperfect
Lives scattered on the internet
the untold truth and salient points revealed
I wonder now how long
that I have left
This year I will turn eighty-five
and I'll do my best
I'll take my vitamins
and read the *New York Times*
and do the crossword
Try to emphasize what's
truly valuable—I'll try to
vote for people who are up to it
and get this criminal
gone before I die

24.   Longing

The dangerous lucid hour
Is where I long to go
Betting my life
On a vanished dream
Where the light goes
Deep in the sea
Where love is always a lullaby
To the sound of a far-off train
And the purple flowers weep and bend
At the touch of the soft spring rain
And a golden eagle flies
From the hands of the little child
Over the steps of Mongolia
The place where the dream lives on
While the wild winds blow
And the fox is caught not for its fur but its life
How far should you go
To catch a dream without the hunting knife
In the teeth of a falcon's beak
From sea to sea, from mountain to mountain
As far as a song can speak

25. Before We're Gone

Stay on the train, the scenery changes
Emerge like a dragon soaring
The skies
There is no end to the things of the heart
As catastrophes open your eyes
Rounding the corners on rickety tracks
I can see the mountains
I never look back
Over my shoulder the angels appear
Fighting the demons that take up
The rear
I expect the best and prepare for the worst
My life is in music, my love is in verse
I'll tell the stories until I drop
I'll drink the nectar, I'll never stop
So bring on the vistas, bring on the views
Bring on the best and the terrible news
We are riding for history, riding for light
Will never give up or turn out the lights
Stay on the train
Till the moon drowns the stars
Till the tracks run out and they close the bars
Blow the whistle and ring the bells
We'll visit the temples and Dardanelles
To hell with the price of living the life
We'll whirl in the dance
And play the fife
The music plays and the train moves on
We'll see it all before we're gone

26.   Joy

An absurd dangerous joy
Came over me that morning
As I slipped down the steps of the castle
And stood in the rainy misty air
Looking at the man in the Levi's and topcoat
He was leaving England
For Denver he said
Running his free hand through his
Damp dark handsome head of hair
That fell back over his eyes
He gave me a look that sent me spinning
It was the end of the beginning

27.   Black Dog

Black Dog chasing me down the halls
Trying to get me down
Black Dog trying to make me fall
Growling around the town
Barking at me from the shadows
Calling me from the hall

Telling me I am nothing, why not die
It is the feeling in my body
This dark snarling fur-covered
Being that lives in me hidden
And unbidden for days for years
And strains at his leash out of nowhere
Tearing chunks out of the woven sweetness
As the sun goes dark

Only at my weakest can he track me here
Only when I'm dreamed out and wept out
And shaken by that sinking sorrow that
Comes in the side door whispering your
Name or my father's dark secret
Or my despair

No name for you but hopeless
No cure for you but time
No reason no booze no drug
Brings you howling in my mind
Nothing but ancestors sobbing their
Duet with you, choruses of tears
Straining their throats
No chains to lock you up
As I have no cure for your rage as I have
No whip to take you down
As I have done before

Down, down, dark canine
Slink away for another few days or years
While I pray and fast and dream and sweat off your memory and leave
you whining
In your hidden corners away from the light
Goodbye for years or a fortnight but
Goodbye all the same

There is no shame here, only you on the run
We are finally done here

28.   Between Midnight and Three in the Morning

The famous, the personal,
the ones who got me through the night,
who harbor my secrets
in their hearts and in their minds,
the ones who are gone and never forgotten,
they all make up my crowd of angels,
my pantheon of memories.
They are forever here
even if they are forever gone,
many with me, many departed—
my pals, my muses, my cherished,
the people I've spent hours with on the phone
getting me through the night—
me getting them through the night
hours, listening to their travels
as I pour mine into the spaces
between sighs and dreams,
between midnight and three in the morning

20.   Todd Beamer
9/11 Flight 93

Some things never get so far into the heart
—this does, in a way few things do—
I thought the tears were over
They are just starting—again
—I was asleep at the moment
Todd was talking to Lisa in faraway Los Angeles
I was awakened to the Towers in smoke and flames
Then all coming down on my city
—I never will be asleep again in the same way
—my God, what have we to do now but weep
God bless you, Todd, up there in that hell in the sky—
Are you guys ready?
Let's roll

30.　In the Present

In the present
All is well
Your death did not occur today
The flowers and the wishing well
Are lovely in the light of May
Tomorrow has no power, no sway
What happens then is not today
The winter day you took your life
Does not confront this sunny now
When all is well makes one more bow
And lifts a glass to this is how
To get through mourning your last breath
And stay in time that is not death
That somewhere in the past
Resides
I know not where and take no sides
I'll stay here where they know my name
Where shadows have no one to blame
Where memories slick with residue
Do not take on a darker hue
The sun shines on in spite of death
In spite of time, in spite of you
I'll stay in now, where no one knows
How desolate the present grows

31.   Secrets of War

The fields in Vietnam are bright as emeralds
The colors iridescent, verdant, pine
Mossy shamrock paddies glow like jewels
Spread across a country old as time

Colors soft and rolling in the rice fields
Shimmering over acres rich with fate
Hollows where the scars will bleed forever
In a peace that always seemed to wait

In 1996 I went to Hanoi
The city welcomed me with open arms
The verdant rice fields sparkled green and emerald
The girls in silken dresses quaint with charms

The war was over and the rice was growing
The bicycles were thick as tangled rhymes
Forgiveness like a gentle wind surrounds us
The tea was sweet, the faces old as time

When I went to Paris for the peace talks
Americans received us with their frowns
A hundred of us tossed upon their consciences
They dreamed that they could drive us out of town

While bombers strafed the green and verdant paddies
The rice fields and the cities old as sin
While opium pipes in Saigon burned like pyres
The embassy of Diem let us in—

South Vietnam gave us tea and sympathy
They said it was for sure that they would win
They spoke to us as children in the nursery
Who can't be trusted with the guns and gin

In Washington the generals were talking
As though this war was something they could win
As soldiers lost their minds there in jungles
And waited for the horror to begin

Our little group was small and you could pity
Our vain attempt to lay it on the line
We were so few and all that day in Paris
The rain would fall; the sun would never shine

Then we visited another country
In Paris, those who fought above Hanoi
The Vietnamese embraced us with a party
That night we had a curious sense of joy

And there we were—we pleaded to the diplomats
The ones who gave us parties or who'd not
The stories we were told were all concocted
The process was a ploy, a fake, a plot

The president shadow-danced while men were dying
In those jungles green and red with blood
Dying at the mercy of the government
Rotting in the rain and in the mud

They fought with Genghis Khan, they fought with China
They fought Japan for years and fought with France
It must be something in the shimmering rice fields
That makes them heal from wars out of the past

Perhaps the Buddha lives among the paddies
Where people know how time and tide can fly
I hope I learn to feel their faith in healing
I hope I learn to let the past go by

I hope I learn how green the grass can shimmer
I hope in living long that I can try
I hope that I can plant the seeds of heaven
I yearn to learn that hope can never die

       Secrets of the war are in the postscripts
       Stories that are written bright with blood
       Horrors of a war are in the body
       Terrors of the jungle and the mud
       We may question on and on forever
       Tears for those who never said goodbye
       Tears for those who never said goodbye

32.   Chopin

What I forgot to say in the interview
That went on and on
With those wonderful women
The Soul Sisters on the radio
About myself and my father and his music
And the Great American Songbook
I talked about my suicide attempt and the alcoholism
And growing up in an alcoholic family
And many other things I didn't mention that are
Fundamental
What I forgot to say was
There was always classical music
On the record player
Chopin, a lot of Chopin, and Debussy and
Respighi, the *Pines* and *Fountains of Rome*
The great composers, played often by Horowitz—
There was much more than the great American
Composers
And the great Irish ballads—
But amidst the Maids of Constant Sorrow and the
Songs of Woody Guthrie were the great Chopin Ballades
and the unaccompanied Cello Sonatas played by Casals
There were the talking books,
My father called them,
From the Library of Congress
And Judith Anderson and Ralph Richardson
Reading *The Cocktail Party* by T. S. Eliot and
All the time—beauty all around us
And I survived it all—

33.   Grand Lake

When I can't sleep
I go back to the mouth of the
Colorado River in the summer of '58
when the fish turned up their silver undersides
for two weeks and the pine trees swung up overhead
and the lake was smooth as silk
when I fell off the water skis
and rough with big waves when I skied well
I go back to ironing the sheets
and cleaning the cabins
and playing the guitar and singing the old songs
And the handsome guy
from the stables in Grand Lake
would come by on his gelding
with the soft leather saddle
on a paint with a lariat
and he would whistle to the screen
in the room where I was dressed and ready
in my boots and soft leather shirt
It was called jingling, and we would
ride up to the meadows
where the horses had spent the night
in tall, green, miraculous grass
and we would herd them on our mounts
down to the stables in town
And by then I am peacefully,
quietly, soundly asleep, horses riding in the meadows
All's well with the world for a few hours this night

34.   Gene Hackman Has Dinner

I saw this splendid actor once
sitting alone during the holidays
in a New York City diner
his head moving up and down
over a plate of what I'm sure was
the specialty of the day
I didn't want to bother him of course
and for years I've regretted that I didn't say hello
Who is the painter who does the scene
in the diner through the window
of the guy sitting there talking to the waiter—
it's a bleak picture, a sad picture
and as I am on the road much of the year
traveling sometimes by myself
and often eating my breakfast
and lunch alone in a hotel
I know the feeling Gene Hackman
must've had—the crew of the movie
that he was making
was probably off somewhere
and he was probably on his way to a hotel
It's a plumb lonely feeling
and I would hope that if someone sees me
hunkered over the special of the day
they might drop a quick hello
at least in memory
of Gene Hackman's solitary dinner at the diner

36.   Acquaintances

The ones we've known since childhood;
the ones we've seen in portrait galleries;
the ones we've met up with briefly
across a crowded room
in some exotic encounter
that we write of in our journals;
the ones our mothers met
when they were young and free
and devouring the culture
and the presence of new friends
in new cities,
some of whom were famous;
the ones our uncles knew;
the ones we dreamed of meeting;
a few are gathered here beneath this canopy
           of time in memory

36.   Richard Fariña

It was 1960, summer
I was living with my first husband
My starter husband Pete
My friend Richard Fariña was married to Carolyn Hester
And they had rented a place on Martha's Vineyard
        with a lake and a garden
Richard said, "Come stay with us"
"Bring your bathing suits and not much else"
We loaded Clark—
Our year-and-a-half-old baby—
And Peter's younger sister Hadley
Into our Chevy carryall
And headed for the north shore from Connecticut—
On the ferry
To the Vineyard, we squinted into the sun
        and ate potato chips and drank Cokes
And bobbed on the sea
Richard met us on the dock, Carolyn in tow
They were brown as two nuts, eyes sparkling, long hair
Prince and Princess, folk royalty
They piled into our Chevy and
Richard said
"We have a surprise for you"
We drove through spartan, tourist-filled Edgartown
Where the flower boxes were full of purple flax and
Wild red and pink roses
And stopped at a quaint shop—
In the window surrounded by seashells
And piles of T-shirts with logos of the Vineyard
And watercolors of ships and children
        with buckets of sand was a
Hand-painted sign

Carolyn Hester and Richard Fariña
With Special Guests
Bruce Langhorne
&
Judy Collins

I nearly fainted
Richard grinned and giggled and looked at me guiltily
"I couldn't help it," he said—
   "a way to wipe out your expenses"
I grinned too—
We always grinned at Richard's antics—
Then, and when he was married to Mimi Baez
And tossed the roasted turkey out the window
Into the snow in Cambridge on Thanksgiving night
For a joke
And when he would sing his songs to me—
"Hard-Loving Loser" and "Pack Up Your Sorrows"
Which he wrote
With Joan's older sister Pauline—
And on his sudden visits to New York
Where he would stay over at my
Upper West Side apartment and we would go shopping
At Zabar's and Dick would put smoked
Salmon on his head
We did sing the surprise show in Edgartown—
Carolyn with her lovely high notes
And Richard playing his sweet dulcimer
—bells in sunlight and

Me singing while Bruce,
   sweet and talented man, played his guitar
The little crowd did their best
   and then we drove to Richard's rented cabin on the lake to
   sleep

Late that night we all heard something go bump
Out sprang Bruce with the rifle provided
        by the landlord of said cabin
He shot a perfectly
Stunned rabbit
Who provided our dinner of rabbit stew
        "à la Hester" the next night
Which we ate
After a day of messing about with the
Rowboat—also provided by the landlord
There was only one other boat on the lake—
At least a mile away on the other side
Of that little lake—
And somehow we managed to run into it,
        hitting it broadside
With many screams of
"Look where you're going!"
And "I don't believe this!"
At the oars, Richard couldn't stop
Little damage was done
        except to neighborly relations
Home at last we could laugh about it all
And remember it as one of the very best times
We ever had
Go figure—we must all be slightly crazy
Like Fariña, my dear and beloved friend
Who drank too much at his book party for
        Been Down So Long It Looks Like Up to Me—
Five years later when he was married to Joan Baez's
Youngest sister Mimi
Fariña got on the back of a motorbike
He was killed at midnight when the guy driving hit a
Sharp turn
Richard flew into eternity that night
And I still dream about him

Sometimes It's Heaven

And about Martha's Vineyard
They had been
Truly wonderful times
Always magical with Richard
I still miss him
And his kind of crazy

37.　I'm Over You

For Gertrude Stein

I'm over you
I'm not over you
I'm over you
I'm not over you
I'm over you
I'm not over you
I never was over you
I'll get over you
I won't get over you
I can't get over you
I'll never get over you
I'm over you
I'm not over you
Never

38.   Ruined Gamblers
After the Vanished Velázquez

The ghosts of ruined gamblers
The pain of vanished lovers
The quiet in the violence
And the silence in the storm
The feeling when you're flying
And you know you're only dreaming
The quiver of the music, the bright morn

The whirling of the dervishes
That dance among the shadows
The memory of that winter
When your carelessness was born
The kisses that we gave away
When yearning for lost lovers
We never had the heart for anyway

When it all came down to truth
We saw a smile that beckoned
From the boat out on the river of our youth
We hitched a wagon to the team
That pulled us to a mountaintop
Surviving breathless visions in the air
We saw the stars that blazed away
And dipped behind the moon
The stranger as he tiptoed down the stair
The creek that ran along the hill
Full of silver trout
Flashing in the water like the stars
As the earth slid down the sun
To block the light again
The vanished stories found in our memoirs

39.   The Dangerous Ones

The dangerous ones always got me
The ones with that glint in their eyes
The ones who would break you and make you believe
Then leave you and dare you to cry
The ones who climbed mystical mountains
Spent nights in the freezing cold rain
The ones who would follow some heart to the grave
And swim through their rivers of pain
The ones who wrote poems and love songs
The ones who would vanish like smoke
The moment you told them you loved them
They'd take all your laughter and hope

And then I found you and your courage
You stayed when I wanted to run
No mysteries now and no shadows
No yearning for dreams that are gone
I love you for being my dragon
I love you for being my sword
I love you for being my lover
I love you for trusting my word

40.   Guns

In high places and low gutters,
Ruby-paneled palaces and dark street corners,
In offices and on the beaches, in every century,
        in slaughter by mass decree,
The brutality of the trenches
        and the sophistication of high office,
Guns are used to solve everything.
        On the streets, in the parks and the schoolyards,
In the kindergartens, the high schools,
        the offices of the manager
Who was recently fired
        and furious about everything on the planet;
In the bedrooms of the millionaire;
        outside the slaughterhouse;
Beside the limousines
        and aimed above the heads of children;
In drive-by shootouts
        that can kill the child who's in the way;
By the officer in a hurry
        with his gun loaded,
Murdering an unarmed civilian
        fighting for his life on a dark sidewalk;
By the slow, wide river
        that slides on toward the sea
With its burden of corpses
        from the shootout a week ago;
Intentional or accidental,
        planned and surprising, held in secret;
Locked in the closet
        in the box above the bedroom slippers;
Standing tall in the corner in the kitchen,
        loaded; sitting in innocence
On the table by the glass
        beside the whiskey bottle;

Near enough to the voices that rise in anger
        on a Saturday night after quite a few drinks
And that party at the club—
        after which he has his hand around her hair and
Stumbles around the bed and reaches for the gun.
        In the schoolyards, in the schoolrooms,
By the water fountain,
        in the lunchroom,
In the hallways, through the doors
        of the chemistry lab
Where a little boy dies on the floor
        with blood pouring across the room,
His brother huddled over his dead body
        among shards of glass—
In the closet of a teenager
        who has gone viral on Facebook
And social media to say he's going to murder every one of
        his classmates.
In the high-powered rifles
        and rifles with bump stocks
And the perpetual roll
        of bullets that never end,
Roaring into the crowd at a
        mass music festival in Las Vegas
Out a window of a hotel room
        with soundproof glass.
        Guns—
In rage and anger and frustration,
        in military action, in trouble—in drama,
In high-wire tension,
        in guilt and innocence,
Time marches on, loaded with bullets
        and ready to fire.

41.   Saint Paul

It always seemed to take me
such a long time to St. Paul
Time always seemed to stand still
I'd finally see the river
the cathedral on the hill
where you and I would walk
The golden carriage atop the capitol
still looks over the Mississippi
where your ashes drifted
We sent them downstream
on a rainy night one November
        thirty years ago
The city in which you died
was named after Saul, who became
Saint Paul on the road to Damascus
He changed his mind
Everyone changes their mind
        Even you, my beloved

42.   Eternal Waters

We threw flowers in the river
red carnations purple roses
flowers floating by the ashes
from your journey through the fire
Ashes in the water with
the roses and carnations
Dust to water dust to dust
in the current of the river
drifting down beside the cities
with the roses and carnations
purple roses red carnations
on the way down to the ocean
Flowers in the ashes
and the ashes in the water
Red and purple
in the water of the rivers
and the dust
Dust to dust and dust to ashes
in the waves of the Atlantic
in the rivers of our childhoods
        on the mighty Mississippi
Red and purple flowers floating
All are headed to the waters
to the surfs of California
to the men in wetsuits riding
through the red and purple flowers
On the waves above your ashes
and the flowers and the water
in the dust of you
not living
No longer are you surfing
No longer are you swimming
No longer are you singing
No longer are you flowering
Red and purple like the flowers

Sometimes It's Heaven

that linger here
when you have the rivers
      and the oceans you have swum
and the waves of oceans near you
and the flowering all around you
forever floating in eternal waters
      You are here

43.   Blood and Ashes

Last night I heard the nightingale was singing
A unicorn went flying through my dream
My open arms were full of bougainvillea
A blue kingfisher flew above the stream

The sun glanced off his wings and sparkled silver
His eyes were iridescent in the light
I watched him flying out over the river
And heard his voice call through the darkest night

I must have dreamed of paradise undaunted
Amidst the war that rages at my door
The shouting and the angry voices calling
The hate unleashed by devils wanting more

Rage has fired the guns but not with roses
Someone in the attic heard the moan
An eagle with his wings of blood and ashes
Cries all alone—his sky is gone

Some say please do something yes do something
Already it may just be far too late
Others say no no you must do nothing
It's only just a dream or it is fate

I stand here as you go on with your dreaming
While a nightmare spreads his awful wings
Defeat him for he comes here to destroy you

The nightingale is weeping as she sings
          The nightingale is weeping as she sings

44.   Singing Heart

At seventeen my heart rose, celebrating
As we hurtled down the Rocky Mountain road
Out of Denver with my dreams of Mozart
And Woody Guthrie shining through the miles
Columbines and hummingbirds in whispering pines
Swallows swooping over crystal waterfalls
At dusk bright wings were glistening in the twilight
Purple-green whispering through the night
Dreaming of the day when I could chase the light

My heart rose up, flying like a sparrow
Over the golden fields and prairies wide
Never satisfied, I bet on pleasure
Seeking treasure, I could never hide
Growing wings for speed, for sleep, for love
Toward the bright lights on the rainy streets
Kisses in the moonlight, love's forever
Moonbeams in my never-ending prayers
Centuries ahead like breaking headlights
Save the planet, save yourself
        Be brave

Sing for all the pain behind the pleasure
Sing for all your worth
It will set you free

45.   Leonard and the Lover

That winter of '74, I took my lover
To meet Leonard Cohen
The wind raged around the corner at the
Chelsea hotel, and the snow howled in
The doorway, blowing our coats
As we stood between glass and ice,
Memory and eternity
The air in the room was tense
I wanted Leonard to
Bless my new lover,
But like a dazed lover myself—
Something I knew Leonard
Understood—
I wanted his blessing untainted
The sun came out and the
Snow melted and the wind died
And then, many years later, so did
Leonard. I thought he would never die
But, like that love affair and the wind and
Life at the Chelsea,
All would come to an end.
The lover and I are still living,
Although not together;
We still write, and we still remember
That day at the Chelsea
When Leonard approved, smiling in that
Sly smile of his, smoothing his calm voice
As he always has and always will
Over my anxious heart
As we stood between glass and ice,
Memory and eternity

46. Death Be Damned

For William Carlos Williams

I love you
beyond the veil of tears
the shades of night
that hide my eyes from looking
down the shaft that leads to death
Without you
I never feared to die
but not to be here with you
has ruined death for me
that once reached out its arms
of folded care
The soft embrace
The end a gentle space
I now scream no
across the waves
across the years
across the river of our intertwining lives
that flows in dreams and in my blood
I do not give a damn for death
No not this time
Across my living breathing soul
I reach for you I will not die
and leave you here to love alone
        So death be damned

47.   The Sunken Road of Fredericksburg, 1863

The trees—
Pines and oaks
Dogwood, crabapple
Cypress, beech
Birch, elm, hemlock and maple
Purple blossoms winding
Through the green leaves
Like lovers' arms
Draped against one another
Like the men in blue and gray
Swaying toward Fredericksburg
Captains, lieutenants, privates, colonels, generals, freed slaves
And unfree

The wretched, the wicked
The brave, the weary
The rested, worn-out
Patriots cleaning their guns
Saying their prayers
Under the branches
Of green trees yearning
To Fayetteville
Great great great great
Enlisted grandfathers
Young fathers
Forefathers
Rufus and George
Preparing to fire
Preparing to die
In the war
Fighting for Stonewall
For Grant
For the Union
For freedom
Under the trees

Sometimes It's Heaven

Holding the birds
And soldiers in
Their arms
Blood at their roots
Blood of my forefathers
Byrds and Collinses
Coldwells and Copes
The burden of time
Proof of life
Till death do us die
Fighting to live
Under the trees of Fredericksburg
These beautiful bloody
Bayoneted
Beyond redemption, trees
Still bending toward
The peace of Fredericksburg

48.   Unrequited Love

In the canyons of bright childhood
Came a knight in shining armor
With his sparkling sword and buckler
Strode across the grassy mountain

Carrying the message forward
To his captain in the dark woods
Message from a girl of twenty
Who was searching for her lover

He had gone into the wild woods
Hoping for the badge of manhood
And was cut down like a sapling
Marching from Saint Paul to Gander

She had dressed in silk and violet
And her feet were clad in silver
All her tears were watering heaven
She had seen the heart go flying

Off into a thousand countries
Trying there to find her lover
And to see if he were living
In the woods the knight stood watching

As she came nigh with her letter
Slowly she could see his armor
Nodding near the rushing river
Ringlets curled down from her forehead

And her tears ran through her fingers
She forgot that he was going
So this letter never reached him
She wrote that she never loved him

Then she knew that he lay dying
And her heart did break forever
Send this letter so he reads it
While his life is slowly ebbing

In the dark earth where he's laying
Tell him that her heart was lying
Love was never unrequited
Rushed into her heart his passion

Slaying her within the hour
Of his dying breath and whisper
Tell him she will always love him
And he rose to go on living

So if you should have a letter
That you have not sent for heartache
See you send it out this minute
To the one you know who loves you

Dress in violet and ribbons
Dress in silk and maybe satin
Blue and red and green and purple
So you seem to be a rainbow

In the canyons of bright childhood
Came a knight in shining armor
With his sparkling sword and buckler
And he crossed his heart forever

49.   The Saints' Birthday

Down on the roadway under
The greening trees
They march in formation
On the saints' birthdays

Eyes like lovers
Dewy with lovers' tears
Like men you knew
A girl with her heart on her sleeve

Their coats are sewn with
Stripes of gold and silver
Invading armies
Dreaming of revenge

The smoky fires along the ridge
Mark boundaries beyond
Which they do not venture
Imagining the very worst

In the trees the violet eyes are watching
The saints have left for palaces near mountains
The girls are in the
Unforgiving fountains

My lips are sealed
I am the captain's daughter
And only I know
How to stop the slaughter

50.   Twilight Ruins
            For A

Your voice brings all we've left behind
To light again
And hovers in the branches of the piñon trees
The shivering shadowed
Passage of the moon
And in the starlight under water
Where forgotten dreams
Shiver with the memories of holy days
Mountain passes half-remembered music
Winding through the bloodlike rivers
Rolling past the columbines
And purple-painted hills
Pouring over the marble cliffs
Where light danced through the caverns
And sank in splendor down your
Sunlit memories
Nothing lasts, everything remains
To taunt and heal, to sway and hold the past
As close as your first breath, your first cry
Across the fields as summer
Moves the wheat in golden rows
The light of other seasons draws the rain
You brave it with your voice
In hollows made from shafts of jewels
Falling from the sky like glints of heaven
Lifting us to clouds of bright beginnings
And endings we had never planned to live for
And time that finally found us
Though nothing lasts and everything remains
As close as twilight ruins
Sunlit memories
And promises you never meant to keep

51.   Savage God

Linwood Avenue
Trees flanked the street
Minnesota winter
shivering under the snow
Tire tracks to the garage
where the Subaru
jumps into life
Champagne bottle
popping open
Crack of light
from the three o'clock afternoon sun
through the space under the door
Always meant to fix that
Too late now
Turn on the tape recorder
Hook the handcuffs onto the
steering wheel
The doors shut—locked tight
Too late to change my mind now
Too late
The voice from a quarter of a century ago
on his death tape
It's taking so long
This champagne sucks
I love you Mom
So sorry honey
Your drawing is so beautiful
I love you
Goodbye
You savage God
I did not mean this
But this is how it ends

52.   Heaven and Earth

The rugged red folds of the Grand Canyon,
the mountains of Northern California with that
soft, rounded look of buff-greens and faded yellows
      —the ones my sister paints
in those yearning paintings—
telling me I have missed something vital—
and there is no way to get it back,
not without moving heaven and earth,
and then where would I go? How would I live
out there by myself, or in the
Grand Canyon, on the banks of the rushing
Colorado River as it carves
the canyons as it always has—
you can't really have a house there on the river.
The Park Service would throw you out
and there you'd be again, homeless and yearning.
So I stay looking down from the jet,
my heart aching as I read my paper
and do the crossword and
search for the power cord
which I seem to have lost on the last plane,
my ticket safe in my purse,
heading for another place
I will see very little of,
though it is beautiful and powerful
and full of brilliant purple shadows between
the shoulders of the smaller,
older mountains in Arizona,
where I will stay only two nights
and sing with the orchestra. When I sing
I go to those places that I am
unable to find in real life—
I drift to the rugged
Rocky Mountains in Colorado and
I walk through the bright columbines

that dot the spring meadows around Boulder
where I once lived,
and I ski—oh, how I ski!—
down the silvery white powder
of snowdrifts in the Rockies, in a storm—
I prefer skiing in snowstorms,
with the Douglas firs beside me
in their white powder dresses,
and I scream with delight
and shout and breathe in deeply
and make my turns with
my skis tight together
as I was taught—old-school—
I think of my youngest brother, Denver,
who skied so beautifully,
the most beautiful skier I have ever seen.
Heaven and earth,
that's what it takes,
that's what it is.

53.   Wounded Birds

Wounded birds in San Francisco
Living on the street
Beggars at the highway corner
Praying just to eat

Lying under rags and paper
Sleeping in the cold
You can't get much for nothing
And you're getting old

Much too old to fight the system
Not too old to care
Too worn out with no job waiting
So damn sick to dare

There's the Midnight Mission waiting
Out there in LA
With some help of heaven they can
Speed them on their way

On the Bowery there are places
You can go to try
Helping hands to hold your own
You might reach the sky

Romance just the nearest light that
Shines outside your door
More than this we cannot do
Just settling the score

54.   Charleston

There are fountains in the garden
And the church is full of blood
Of the innocent and unsuspecting
Dying in the flood
As the young man with the gun
Runs forever down the stairs
Into the glowing fire of our prayers

There are fountains in the garden
They are shedding crystal tears
There is sunlight in the Plaza
And the suddenness of fears
There are silver shadows bending
In the rose Crepe Myrtle leaves
As nine innocents are slaughtered
While we grieve
In the history of Charleston there is
White and black and fear
There's the scent of former royalty
And murder in the square
There are mummers in the chapel
There is thunder in the air
There's the tale of what men do
And what they dare

There's the story of a warrior
The story of a king
There's the fragrance of mimosa in the shade
There's the rice and there's the cotton
There are ships and there is war
There is blood and there are fortunes to be made

And the people who survived the
Murders take a different road
They are praying for the killer
Where the bloody river flowed
They are kneeling to find comfort
From the God who is their hope
They are looking for the spiritual
And even for the pope
There are fountains in the garden
It is June of '17
And the killer has been captured and the
Aisles have been mopped clean
Of the blood of all the murdered
Who are buried in the ground
And the sun still shines and
Some forgiveness found

There is sunlight in the Plaza
Shining on crepe myrtle trees
But the guns are never silenced and
The bullets not retrieved
For they fly in other cities in the years that
Come to pass
And these killings never stopped
And so alas
And so alas

55.   There in the Deep

They're dropping like flies, I said to a friend
The ones I loved, the ones I loathed
The rich and famous, weak and mild
The one with blazing hair and not a care
The one who smiled at me
And brought me flowers
They will fulfill their share of hours
And heave into that
Hearty dark that takes us all
The wren, the lark, the singing bird
The hounds of prey, the haunted ones
The maids of May
The brutal and those in silken gowns
The smiling ones, the
Queens and kings
The ones who have no homes, no rings
No shattered dreams
No hats to wear.
So have a care to listen to the songs of
Praise, the dreary days, the sunlit dreams
The shadows and the passing things that
Seemed so vital to the play
My youngest brother
Fine and rare and beautiful
A magic flower in the garden of my life
I know I cannot live without him
But must, all dust to dust
Patricia, Jane, and Doris
And now the other day came
Lorna, beloved by Mother Teresa
Auctioneer to the world and Sotheby's
The day will come when there's no time to pray within
This play, when all is laid aside
All worry and all fratricide, all smiles
And all the clothes you wore

All peaceful vigils, tools of war
Outside the bedside where we die
There is the sky and memories of those who rise
Like phantoms in the cloudy sky
To weep and pray and keep the secrets or
Display them far and wide, for all to peer at
All will see, there is no shame, no greed in death
No afterthoughts no breathing and no
Fond regrets, for all is done
The weeping and the fun, the nighttime and the sun
The blaze of love, the daring feat.
There is no cheating death, no afterglow, no
Firelight, no shades of pity or of hurt.
This is the end, the just deserts
The time of counting up the score
Of words well said, of nothing more.
And nothing less than death
It's on its way, no matter what we say
Or slow the clock upon the mantelpiece
Like Tristram Shandy
Turn the hands back here and there
Back instead of forward, as he did
All's fair in love and death
No more to love no more to see the hands go by.
No time to yield, no time to cry.
Fierce death and gentle sleep
All will come, all will come
No scores to keep
There in the deep.

56.   Scripture

The scripture of landscape
Better than preaching
Better than singing
Better than praying
Better than church
Life of the walking
spirit of mountains
Sun on the pine trees
Diamonds in water
Oh, for the Rockies
Oh, for the memories
Tail of the red fox
The mirage of marten
The flick of the antelope's
coat in the sunlight
Sparkle of eyes
as we reached the summit
Those days in the mountains
on the virgin lake
by the sparkling water
Make my heart break
They go so fast, these
days in the wilderness
Marked by the breathing
Drenched by the tears
Longing for daybreak
Gone with the years

57.   Sober 31

Wernersville, PA, from LaGuardia
on the earliest flight in human history
Got off the plane somehow at the
right airport, lily white
dark as night, sick as a dog
Let it all go
Who wouldn't have taken bets against that—
Already drunk
Slugged down the vodka from the jelly glass
in the airport when we landed in the
hills of Pennsylvania and my life was over
7:30 a.m. on a Friday, the nineteenth of April
       Forty-seven years ago
No going forward
No turning back
Tulips purple and white in the driveway
to the farm and peeking out of the
black soil around the windows of my room
in detox, bright orange and red—
Had not seen a bright flower
or had a bright idea in years
There were things that looked OK
on the outside of my life
if nobody knew the truth
Suitcase of books and pills
dropped at the door
I shimmied into
paper slippers—a real star
The nurse looked at me and smiled
And said, "Why don't you let us drive?"

58.   Among the Dying

In those old days we drank the way we breathed
We sat beneath the willow trees and sang
The lyrics spoke and we were young as spring
September far off as a bluebird's wing
My hand was always closer than your heart
When we were bound together like the river
That wound beneath the windows of our tower
And murmured that the gift was with the giver
Our lives were lived by dreams and by the hour
Sweet century that flowed by like a dream
We took our time with pleasure and with pain
I loved you in the wind and in the rain
And knew somehow I'd not see you again
But many days I listened to our hearts
Declaring that we'd never be apart
Declaring we were there for war and art
And knowing that we'd never really start
Because the war was burning through our lives
And gave us just one chance to stay alive
Among the dying

59.   Switchback

It all started in Georgetown
Wearing those Justin boots
Sometimes I think it ended
Just about a mile from the roots
From the very beginning
Things were locked up tight
We skied all day at Arapahoe
And had our very first night

This is the field where it happened
Where the buffalo roamed all day
Finally finding their way home
Beyond the sun's last ray
Here is the place where we two sat
Feeling our pain to the bone
Knew it would lead us somehow
We would never be alone

Drove till we finally ran out of road
With no map of where we'd go
Independence Pass and Sinatra
Carrying a heavy load
Genesee Park lay at our feet
We never knew the luck of home
All the wild grass was blowing
I was suddenly all alone

Tried making it up the mountain
In a storm of snow so free
Woke up at just around daylight
And knew I was finally me
Hooray for the wide-open spaces
Mountain peaks have no peer
Then another round of switchbacks
Try to do away with fear

One more dance with the devil
One west, one running east
Where we would land no one knew
There was famine, there was feast
Today I can see my younger self
Riding in that sleigh
One more dance with the devil
Leading to today

60.   You Know Who You Are

You know who you are
Flying like a bright light through my dreams
Waking me at midnight
To your face above mine
Looking out at me
From the window of the train
From the bank of clouds above Mount Shasta
For the third time this morning—
While the phone is ringing
While the shower is splashing
While the light is changing
While my toast is burning
While my eyes are yearning
You know who you are
I have sought you in the crowd of faces
In every horse that races
For the finish line
In every dream that finds me on
The trail that winds through valleys blossoming
With violets and columbine
In tides and time
In light and darkness, in joy and sorrow
You know who you are

61.   Leonard's Dance

He wore a suit and tie the day he died
Working on another of his songs
One about the future and the past
One that sang of hope when all was dashed

Some say till you've given up the fight
You will never sleep the livelong night
Flashes of your unforgiven sin
Moments of uncertainty fly in

Times of deep injustice will prevail
You will never live until you fail
We have just the moment when we smile
We have nothing left but guilt and style

Why not sing your treasures so they shine
Why not revel in your fragile mind
No one else can take you on this ride
So just give it up and swim the tide

Dress up just as Leonard did to die
Say your kind hellos and sweet goodbyes
So the world has finally understood
Everyone is headed for wormwood

But the sky is up there every day
Wandering from rain to sunny skies
Let the darkness deepen in your heart
So the light can shine upon your art

Sanctify the moment when we part
Cherish all the lightness at the start
Whether it's romance or a crusade
Do your best and dance in the parade

Sometimes It's Heaven

Seldom do you find the gold you seek
Dig for all your worth into the creek
Rivers flowing by take every turn
Through the willows, through the sheltered fern

So wear a suit and tie and walk the walk
There is more to life than sleepless nights
Leonard let his lyrics fall like sand
Let us know the future is unplanned

62.   Paradise

Paradise is ruined and the angel weeps
Lost in the rains of a million tears
Gathering pearls while the sad world sleeps
Through the thunderous storms of these years

Beautiful in all her loss
She plucks the harp, her spells to ply
The bell, the flowers, and the cross
Surrender in the diamond sky

She sings the song that brings the dawn
She mends our hearts with threads of gold
She brings back every dream that's gone
She brings the hope that was foretold

I yield to all her beauty fair
I seek her in the near skyline
She is renewed like summer air
Reborn, refreshed, resolved, refined

Move on, she sighs, we are not lost
Your dreams of freedom must be heard
Across the snows, amid the frost
The eagle, now the soaring bird

Will dig his talons into thieves
Who take the bright-voiced joy you knew
He'll right the wrongs that make us grieve
And give us all the hope that's true

Or take us back to start again
To mend the ragged hearts of men
To seal the sacred promise thus
And carry on, for so we must

63.   Suicide

The snow is beautiful
Falling, swirling, blowing
Dancing, plunging
Flakes as big as divinity
And all along the mountain roads
The ice receives and
Sanctifies the wind-filled sleet
And piles the drifts six feet deep
Along the glassy sheen
Oh god of snow and heartache
The beauty of your face
Smiling on the powdered mountain
In January, month of your birth
And death
My feet still on the slopes turning
Speeding
Tight turns
Headlights bright
Leading me home
Did you get home at last
Past the jagged peaks and valleys
Of winter
I am keeping my feet together, ankles flexible
Eyes wide for the turns
My heart beating like yours
When it stopped

64.   Purple Heart

Coming into Dallas from
The airport
Twisting my head from the car
Where is it? Where am I in relation?
Fifty-five years in time? Half a century
And more?
Is it over there by the shiny
New skyscraper
Tucked in beside the old railroad lines?
Over by the mission
Where the homeless man waits through days
For the sound of the gun to explode
And for a hand to help him
By the flying traffic
Like junk left on the road
There to be polished to a sparkle?
But it's not on this beat
It's buried in me so deep
The place the time the street
The broken brain
The broken head
The blood the future and the past
The prince the king iconoclast
I do not believe the popular lie and
I will not till I die
Until the last
Until death do us part
The country's purple heart

65.   Break of Light

Winter mornings on the ski lift
Cigarette smoke through the pines
Drifting through the white boughs leaning
In the air the sound of chimes
Hot tub full of smiling faces
Lighted by the moon's own rays
Jackets made of down and starlight
Fashioned in our measured days

Light from candles, gathered family
Stories from the first to last
Silken dresses in the snowstorm
Weddings up on Berthoud Pass
Nights of drinking, loud carousing
Falling down in drunken haze
Morning's retribution lingers
Through the holy nights and days

Vail Pass in a sudden snowstorm
Soft like flakes and hard like drugs
Two skis bumping down the highway
Nothing on my feet but Uggs
Longing, lingering, losing, lusting
Fall and summer, winter, spring
Jugs of wine and ropes of cheese
Harmony in songs we sing

Colorado in the springtime
Columbines in each crevasse
Paintbrush shivering in the gusts
Calling bluebirds in the grass
Hot black Chillys stretched on thighs
Shaking into year-old tights
Sweating under polar fleece
And ripping down the snowy heights
Down to fires burning brightly

Toddies, guacamole, chips
Shrugging off those furry booties
Making plans for future trips
Maybe next time we won't stay here
It's too far to get the lift
Next year finds us here again—
Easy, if you get my drift
I love skiing in a snowstorm
He loves skiing in the sun
Homeless ski bum loves it icy
He would ski till all was done

Cracking jokes on top of Swingsville
Down I went that sunny day
Spilt like milk upon the face
Broken bones my own soiree
How about that Demerol
Makes the demons take a hike
No more pain for four good hours
What a ride without a bike

Rehab for the metal shoulder
Worked like hell and got it right
Anything is worth the trouble
On the slopes at break of light

66.   Far from Idaho

My father weeping in
His leather chair that night
His grandmother dying
In Idaho
Laurie Booth on the farm
Where the cows were treated well and the
Billy goats and bees were even
Soundly praised
As he wept
I crept into
The room
Where tears were falling
So far from Idaho had he traveled
Blindly following his dreams
To the Rocky Mountains
Laurie Booth had never seen
My father's glass eyes
Sparkling with tears

67.   Mountain Men

For Ernie Kuncl and John Clark
RIP

Both of you are gone
you who flew down mountain trails
through the Colorado snowstorms
on the icy roads to Vail
on the pass to Winter Park
where we drank from skins of wine
and shouted out our laughter
down the slopes and through the pines
as we reveled and we sang
told our stories by the fires
You were men I was a girl
We sent our hearts out on the wires
You were rangers on Longs Peak
bringing hikers through the rocks
swinging ropes to save the wanderers
on the trail of the red fox
In those years upon the mountains
where we gathered up the storms
then our laughter filled the canyons
that the river's mist adorns
You have echoed through my life
You have saved me from the dark
with the memories of our hiking
Rocky Mountain National Park
Like my godfather Holden
you were brusque and brave and smart
and I needed you to guide me
through my shattered broken heart
You drank whiskey like a logger
You both sang among the pines
and you loved like men of honor
knew the trails and knew the signs
I was never meant for marriage

never then when I was young
though there always was that lure
when you leapt into my life
like sparkling rivers sweet and pure
Your lives are like the silken flags
those that wave on Everest's crest
You were wonder
You were power
truly hearts out of the West

68.   Yearning

Always yearning for something
Some far-off place, some dream
Some fantasy, a mystery
That flies above the stream
Upon the harp that plays the tune
The fingers fine and thin
Remembering with their melodies
That beg life to begin

The days of sun on water
Falling through the air
The lover in her silken gown
Her touch, her skin, her hair
The handsome cowboy shadows
Falling on her face
The violet bougainvillea
Soft dark-purple lace

In moonlight on a quiet lake
The heart that sees the past
The echoes of an old, sweet love
The plains so wide and vast
I yearn for you as starlight falls
Above the violin
The music haunts me as your face
Can seek me through the din

The music plays, the dance is on
My heart in rapture dwells
The tortured memory of laughter
Shatters like sweet bells
And heartache takes me for a ride
Through snowy fields of white
My eyes are open as they see
Too much to bear the sight

69.   Tattoo Parlor

Gladys picked me up in a black SUV
And we drove down the West Side Highway
Two girlfriends talking
Women of a certain age
Tough and at a loss
We talked about our son's lives and deaths
One gets to know quickly there is
Nothing to do about suicide but live through it
And not take one's own life in exchange
There is no guilt
It is mysterious
Horrifying
A nightmare
We talked about our departed boys
About musicals—*Carousel* and Mozart and France and Morocco and
Unicorns
And the horrible things that had happened
When our sons took their lives—
Her Anthony by hanging
My Clark, the motor running
We drove to the tattoo shop
And met Jim, who had tattooed her son
Here in New York
Except when he was traveling to places around the world
Tattoo artists from Manila and China and Vietnam and Italy and
France and Germany and England and South America had tattooed
him with flocks of spangled flamingos
And girls with overblown lips and splendid thighs and eyes
I sat beside my friend watching
While her son's name was etched
Into the flesh that gave birth to him
A melody, a sketch
My son Clark had died by his own hand
When he was thirty-three, the mystical age
I had my son's name tattooed on my wrist

Along with a bluebird—
And perhaps I will spend the next years of my life
Having flowers and birds and fish and rainbows and naked women,
white snow-capped shining mountains and a wilderness of forests
Tattooed all over my body
I will become the illustrated woman
My son would be tickled pink that
His mother has decided on getting tattoos all over her body
As another way to survive his death

70.   Goodman, Schwerner, and Chaney

1964
SDS offices
Sign on the door
Right there on Lynch Street
Struck me as strange
Out there on Main Street
Out on the range
Pickups with gun racks
Fear in the streets
Longing for freedom
Breach of the peace

Great-looking morning
Fog on the hill
Sunlight is golden
Down by the mill

That's where they found them
There by the dam
Dead as you please
They were innocent lambs
Closer to Jesus
Closer to God
Nearer to murder
By firing squad
What are you here for?
Get out of town
Don't look too often
You might get shot down

Look how the future
Comes from the past
Everyone mixing
Together at last
Just like the rainbow

Promised and prized
Medgar's so prominent
Like he's alive
Still gone in terror
Still, he's survived
Fannie Lou singing
Come out and vote
They overcame it
Not a wrong note

Great-looking morning
Fog on the hill
Sunlight is golden
Down by the mill

A half-century out
Tell every story
Walk, sing, and shout
Fannie Lou's here
So don't mess around
What's lost will come back
What's hidden is found
Take it from Jackson
Take it from me
It's not what you think
It's what you can see

Great-looking morning
Fog on the hill
Sunlight is golden
Down by the mill

71   Ancient Warriors
Venice, Italy

My guardian tonight is a stone priest
carved into the wall of an ancient monastery
where the armies of Napoleon held out over Venetian waters
Then a home for soldiers,
a hospital for the wounded,
a city for Fascist warriors
Men have made love to women
in this room,
with its gold-framed paintings
of the Rialto Bridge over the Grand Canal,
the glassworks of Murano,
the vaporetto reflected
in the waters,
and me, where my scrambled eggs and
coffee
have arrived in this twenty-first-century
hotel in Venetian waters
rippling under the same windows
seen once upon a time
by soldiers and priests,
wounded and valiant,
guilty and innocent
And now I see as I gaze out on the water
into the eyes of the stone priest gazing
guilty as some, innocent as others,
trying to live in this world
of water and ancient warriors

72.   Clark's Valentine

The morning before Valentine's
You rang me on the phone
It was raining and a quarter to seven
You said I think
I'm through
I've got to get away somewhere
I said thank God
There must be a god
There's heaven
You'd been to the cathedral
And you got down on your knees
You asked what shall I do
I'll ask my mother
That was me
The winter has been cold
And you'd been sleeping with a gun
I never knew the worst
Of what I knew might happen
You shook the rain out of your hair
And drank your cup of coffee
Black the way you liked it in the morning
Sometimes it's up
Sometimes it's down
Sometimes it's a catastrophe
Sometimes it's wonderful

Sometimes it's heaven
Then it was you and me

73.   Clark's Grammy Marjorie

The golden glow of the gems
In the folds of her silken blouse
The wafting jacaranda
Outside the little house
Under the leafless branches
Of the tree in the warm backyard
The feral kittens were tumbling
Under a sky of stars
You could hear my father singing
And playing the spinet's keys
From the shouting way past midnight
We were given a sweet reprise
The morning coffee flowing
And laughter forced at first
Then down to the beach at Malibu
The waves so unrehearsed
And the little fire we started
As the tide rolled to the shore
Father in his swimsuit
Charging the surf that roared
The smell of the bacon frying
Sizzling in the dawn
I raced the now-incoming tide
Till the morning light was gone
Today I stand by the Ferris wheel
And remember my mother's hands
Waving over the fire
In that long-gone dreamy land
Her wedding ring and her children
Bound her to the shore
That beach in Santa Monica
Where she might have yearned for more
But she loved that crazy blind man
And the children that she bore
She might've dreamed of heaven

And the future at her door
But on the beach the fire burned
And the waves rolled at her feet
All was well in the land of gold
And life was warm and sweet
Years would come when tears were shed
Troubles rolling on
Here in Santa Monica
My mother saw the dawn

74.   Laredo

Down there with the cowboys
I got drunk just like LA
I heard tales of banditos and
Horse thieves
Swam a river of blood
On my way
I ate chilies and talked to the
Wizard
Who gave me a map to get
Home
Peyote and mystical poems
To shield me
As I was alone
I was driving along the mirages
Where the red dog was baring his teeth
So I took out the spell from my pocket
And rocked him like he was a thief
He had the look of a lawyer
The crawl of a man on the make
His disguise as a dog wasn't working
So I took him down fast as a snake
Oh Jesus on the cross
In the bedroom
Where I slept while the
Fire and flame
Stalked the children of
Innocence
In the old violence without any
Shame

75. Singing Like the Dead
For Tennessee Williams

Bits of shattered rainbow
Falling on my bed
Light from diamond windows
What was it you said
Catastrophes succeeding
Not the watersheds
we all thought they were
while building the warhead
Saw the winning races
Watched the thoroughbred
Got down on our knees
Knowing what was in our minds
would likely be unsaid
Praying for the twinkling
of bright stars up ahead
Light beyond the nightmares
Breaking up the dread
Shattered rainbow pieces
Singing like the dead

76. A Sonnet on Love

O love that takes my breath away
That shelters me from fear-dismay
That ties me up and sets me free
And lets me fly and shelters me

O love that has a thousand spears
To pierce the softest heart of tears
Where prayers are deep and all divine
And hold this ancient pledge of mine

Love shines the light into my room
Makes shivering waters in the gloom
Remembers all my saddest nights
And brightens me with gladder sights
There are no bars into my heart
Now love gets in
and tears my life apart

77.   Marjorie

When my mother died
lying in her white bed
with her silvery-gray hair strewn across the pillow
she was at Park Place
in Cherry Creek
so near her home on Marion
four blocks away in Denver
where we gathered and sang and wept
and sprang from our cribs into our Levi's
and then high school
and into trouble
and out of it
and into our lives
She had stood in the doorway with her oldest boy
when the police came and said
he had stolen a car which he parked
very near where he lived
so he wouldn't have to walk very far to find it
My mother said he didn't do it he didn't do it
but he did do it
But then he grew up and did only wonderful things—
When my mother died I was in Florida
I had fallen
flying across the canted stage of another theater
Picking myself up
someone came to tell me
the news that she was gone
What to do when you're so far away
I wept and went on weeping
all the way home to New York
and then to Denver for the funeral where I sang a song
I had written for her and I wept on and off
for the rest of my life so far
And now I see her face
in my own eyes

in my cheekbones
in the way I hold my head in pictures
I bend my hand just so
I see that my fingernails
are absolutely like my mother's
The way she listens to me still
The way she says
you can do it you can do it
And I can do it
And I do it for her
for the rest of my life

78.   Layla

I am finally here
And my black hair—softly straight—
seeming to shine under the fluff
of the pink blanket in which I am
wrapped as my aunties' and uncles'
and my great-grandparents'
and my parents' gazes find me
Lucky beauty
I am born in hard-won peace
the fighting over
most pains things of the past
one hopes and prays
I will drink at my mother's breasts
and lie in her arms
be swaddled
When I open my eyes to look into hers
a quick glance
Almost a wink!
Am I a beauty?
As beautiful
as my mother?
I am Beloved
I know I am
Beloved

79   Burning Desire

I have a burning desire
To take you into my arms
I know it would be a disaster
But feeling it does me no harm
You keep the flame ever burning
By just walking through my door
I am the bird in the window
Waiting and watching for war
In the battle of love I am losing
My poor heart is ticking like mad
I'm broken with longing and yearning
I'm waiting till I can be glad
Lying in wait I am smitten
You drive me wild with your smile
I think I will send you more flowers
Such things are becoming my style
The truth is I'll always be waiting
For you to come into my life
All would be perfect and pleasing
If you'd just divorce your wife

80.   Southern Comfort

Oh, you gave me southern comfort
and you made me feel alive
You were singing like a banshee
in the wind when I arrived
You were brilliant
You were flying
You were giving everything
When I saw you there in Monterey
you had not long to live
We were sitting at the Troubadour
and watching Paulie play
I was drinking like I always did
that night and every day
I was twenty-eight and you were
much too young to fly so soon
You were singing to the masses
You were crying at the moon

Oh, you gave me southern comfort
and you made me feel alive
You were singing like a banshee
in the wind when I arrived
You were dancing on the stage
like some butterfly on fire
You were brilliant
You were flying so much higher
At the break you leaned over
grabbed me by the hand
whispered in my ear
"We should go and meet the band"
Before we stood
you said to me, "One of us will make it"
"It won't be me," you said
and I thought I was mistaken
I knew how much you drank

just like everybody did
but my drinking was so hidden
I was like, "What's that you said?"
Later I was sure I'd heard
her words
as she whirled by
like a flock of singing birds
bound for the sky

Oh, you gave me southern comfort
and you made me feel alive
You were wailing like a banshee
in the wind when you arrived
You were dancing on the stage
like some butterfly on fire
You were brilliant
You were flying so much higher
It was years ago
but still I see it oh-so clear
You were right, for you are gone
and I am here
wondering how you knew
that it would be me
who would make it through the mess
how could you see

Oh, you gave me southern comfort
and you made me feel alive
You were singing like a banshee
in the wind when I arrived
You were dancing on the stage
like some butterfly on fire
You were brilliant
You were flying
You were dying

81.   The Innocence Project

Morning-bright sun
My dream vivid
Only of you
Always of you
I only touched you
Only longed for you
Only imagined
what would happen when
caught
That we splintered after
bonding in the night
Surrounded by light
Running apart like kids under a tree
Carving our initials
when the lightning struck
Running through the rain
Even in a dream of paradise

82.   Flying Lessons

Long after our father had died
My brother Mike was learning to fly
He said he wept
When he flew through the clouds in the sky
And when they parted he saw
What our father had never beheld
The vistas of color and beauty
He had saved the tears
To weep for a man who was blind
In vision but never in mind
After that he looked at the world
As he'd never seen it before
The days were a brilliant surprise
He was filled with the joy of sunrise
Like a panoply spread in the sky
Just to see
        What our father never saw

83.   Ancestors

I dreamed I saw my ancestors fighting on the bridge
Shouldering their rifles in the rain
The ponchos on their backs
As thin and fine as silk
I knew that they were wounded and in pain
One could've been a Collins
One could've been a Booth
As they stood there fighting in the dawn
As they staggered and I watched them
As they fell they could have been
Copes or Byrds for all I knew
They were hurting and their ammunition gone
I prayed that they would make it home
And father one more son
A daughter so I could be born
In some far-future dawn
Dreaming of the renegades
Dreaming of those souls
The women and the men who now are gone
All those men in Fredericksburg
Where springtime trees are bending
All those soldiers fighting in the dawn
For me

84. Shoot the Leg

Hold your fire
Save the guy
Then you will not have to lie
Lose your job and bring much grief
You might feel some sweet relief
Not to mention who you save
You, the trusted and the brave
Did they teach you Taser moves
You don't have a thing to prove
Only that you're not a killer
Looked upon another way
Take the time to reconsider
Think of all the tears you'll save
All the pain and all the rage
If you have to,
Shoot the leg

85.   American Eagle

The sirens are calling
A soft rain is falling
There's blood in the street and it's dawn
They've called the all clear
The rage and the fear
The shadows and ghosts are all gone

The vans with the cops
The lawyers with props
Tried hard to prove all had been legal
Above all the fray
The victim today
Would be the American eagle

The eagle is flying and screaming
And justice is fragilely streaming
In the light of the day
With hell soon to pay
Equality stood redeeming

For above all the fights
The shots in the nights
The ease with which murder was rendered
And everything done
All under the sun
Would seek not to catch the offender

It's catch-22
It's just me and you
And one of us is the wrong shade
They say it's too late
A matter of fate
This has happened since history was made

The eagle is flying and screaming
And justice is hopefully streaming
In the light of the day
With hell soon to pay
Equality must be redeeming

Tonight, there's a guy with a
Light in his eye
He says he will tell how it went down
And suddenly now
There's a change in the how
And why and the when and the meltdown

Somebody finally
got the connection
To what has been happening for years
And now when the press
Goes down through the mess
We might find an answer to tears

The eagle is flying and screaming
And justice is hopefully streaming
In the light of the day
With hell soon to pay
Equality must be redeeming

So find out today
Who's going to say
I did it and now I am sorry
I made some mistakes
I'll take what it takes
We'll abide by the law and the jury

The eagle is flying and screaming
And justice is hopefully streaming
In the light of the day
With hell soon to pay
Equality must be redeeming

The sirens are calling
A soft rain is falling
There's blood in the street and it's dawn
They've called the all clear
The rage and the fear
The shadows and ghosts are all gone

86.   Crystal Hills

Prayer comes easily as I climb the slopes
Penance for the things undone, for vivid hope
Dawn is breaking for me once again in time
I can hear the bells of morning ring their chime

We were trekking in the rocky peaks
We raised up our eyes to see a blazing light
A butterfly of crimson danced in columbine
And thoughts of beauty and of love consumed my mind

We were both so young and all so jubilant
We had come from youth to dreams of long ago
All those years of hoping we could get away
And find another world and live a different way

Sailing down the crystal hill with you my love
Flying past Norwegian pines filled up with snow
My heart so light it rises in the blizzard's wind
And you are closer than the heart under my skin

Dreaming now, my visions coming crisp and clean
Smoke comes out of chimneys from the cabin's lean
Down below is comfort and a fire's blaze
And love and fortune wrap me in their haze

Thanks to heaven for the sweetest days of youth
I will live within their everlasting truth
Lakes and trails and glimmers of the sparkling stars
And the sound of music from the sweet sitars

Give me all the mountaintops for any jewels
Give me time in silence while the snowflakes fall
Love came out of pure thin air from long ago
Followed me from hill to hill, from snow to snow

87.   Any Fool

It's spring
Today my closest friend is going
Daffodils are pouring down the lawn
The coffin draped with roses
Bears the burden
Of youth and friends
And how it was begun
Pictures of the old girl by a river
The fishing line a sparkle in her hair
The stream a silver path as old as summer
We knew she would not hesitate to dare
Her every breath was drawn with quaint conviction
That she would be the one
To never die
The singing in the church
So sweet with harmony
And questions never asked
And never posed
Going out that window
On a Sunday
Forever breathing questions
No one knows
The dawn would come
And any fool would find
That in the daylight
When the heart remembers
We all know
They always change their minds

88.   Northampton Moon

A quarter moon slides north outside my window
The clock strikes three; the trees are almost bare
A winter chill has settled on the city
The night is still and quiet everywhere

Last night I sang my songs in this old village
Where once a poet and a preacher lived
When the countryside was young as pity
Where New England grappled to forgive

Jonathan Edwards and William Cullen Bryant
Lived here in Northampton years ago
One a Christian, one a yearning poet
They must have seen this town in sun and snow

Here in Massachusetts two men struggled
Finding inspiration on the page
Edwards wrote of charity and good works
With an angry God his battle waged

"To a Waterfowl" was written nearby
Bryant's poem to the bird in flight
Windswept through the skies of Massachusetts
Flying with her heart to find the light

I am like that bird the poet wrote of
Flying through the night air like a swan
Winter finding me in songs of twilight
Making toward the moonlight and the dawn

That same power holds my wingtips forward
The one that Edwards preached and wrote about
We all are sinners struggling for forgiveness
In our flight for love, day in and out

Judy Collins

Troubadours like me have always traveled
Hard on roads that wind from high to low
That same moon has seen me gazing at her
As the poet and the preacher know

I wage my battle, melody enshrouded
Singing through the cities far and wide
The sun will rise and I will be a traveler
Searching for the dawns in other skies

We look at the same moon in the night sky
With our joyful songs in fits and starts
Born to travel underneath your brightness
Struggling with our heads and stubborn hearts

You were here when Edwards was a toddler
You were here when Bryant won the prize
You will see me standing by the water
You will see the sorrow in my eyes

Tomorrow will be freezing, say the pundits
Cold and frigid under a bright sun
I will be in other cities like you
Where you'll see me, moon of everyone

Salvation is the answer we were promised
Written in the preacher's words and songs
Poems and the prayers and songs sustain us
To take us from the shores of dark to dawn

Follow me, oh moon up in the heavens
From the winter snows to summer days
Hide me in the shadow of your knowledge
All of us are here under your gaze

89.   Immigration

There are no "others"
Strangers waiting on the brink
Bring us good tidings

90.   Is That You?

We spread the tablecloth
and light the candles
The sun comes up and the light
shines warm upon the
            day through the window
into the room where we gazed
            at the cup and the glass
and the silver
The lamp
It has just turned on suddenly
There was no one there to pull the cord
Is that you?
Here in the room with the candle
            and the cup and the silver
            the glass in the window in the morning
Is that you who is truly gone forever
and yet is always here with me
            and the glass and the cup
and the silver?
Is that you
this night?

91.   Political Freedom

Lake Erie outside my window
The clouds billowing on the horizon
Freighters, schooners
Sailboats with their white hulls
Chicago summer
Sweating in the sheets
Praying for release
Your hands upon the wheel
I thought we had a deal
Lake Michigan so blue so blue so blue
Absinthe in the glass
At the Gate of Horn
Turning yellow in the midnight hours
Drunk on the poetry
Swaying with the music
Guitars in the street
The August heat
My feet tingling
My heart singing
Testifying for the Yippies trial
At their trial, trying to sing
"Where Have All the Flowers Gone"
Judge Hoffman's clerk's hands across my mouth
And Rennie Davis in my bed
After the main event
        In New York
        We made love and talked
        And talked and talked
            Of political freedom

92.   Blue Heron—

The great blue heron flies
with my memories on his wings
In his long sweep over the lake,
into the darkness at the other side,
where the big trees beckon, where light fails,
like him I fly into darkness,
no matter the light, no matter
my struggle with the wind and the water
He is beautiful without effort,
smooth without pretense
Simple lines, bestowed
without strain, without a painting
to commit his loveliness to memory
He floats by the window,
outside a train,
from the roundabout,
Terminal A to E,
outside the rush of wheelies and fast food,
dipping for fish in the still
silver waters off the Florida Keys,
in the far-flung forests of New England
I watch him
in the middle of a Colorado stream,
somewhere outside the Texas ranchlands,
and in his usual haunt, the warmer climes,
he of flight, of dreams
above the house in Connecticut
where he watched me closely, quickly,
easily streaming by into the woods
by the lake where we walked
and watched his plunge and lift,
his eye and wing, his beauty
come and go—
like ours

93. Whip-poor-willl

How much silence
can you bear
What makes time stand still
I'm in the garden by the pond
to hear the whip-poor-will
He's singing out his heart because
he's heard about the war
Where fire streaks the sky and
there's no reason that it's for
He sings, take down the fire
He stretches out his wings
What is all this bloodshed for
and where is God, he sings
Can't you stop the flames
you who look so strong
Everything is broken
It is written in my song
If you only listen you can
hear the sound of waves
beating on some foreign beach
where men are digging graves
Flames light up the burning night in
places in the world
Dancing in the rising sun
dervishes have whirled
Are there any answers to
the clamor of the guns
Still their sound among the reeds
where silver rivers run
First they shut down all the furnaces
that smoked among the ruins
Plant the flowers on the green
and make your retributions
Sing the words upon your lips
Try your hand at peace

Peace among your brotherhood
Violence must cease
Meditate tranquility
Settle on your breath
Remember that the whip-poor-will
will sing you to the depths
across the highest mountains
till his rest

94.   Nez Perce

It was 1910 in Idaho
That a child was born in spring
Under Halley's Comet
Same as young Mark Twain
It's pretty good company
That was all he'd say

Everything that stood
In his way he just outran
He dreamed of flying through the
Great green pine trees
Wearing beaded moccasins like
Jewels on his feet
At the deaf and blind school in Gooding, Idaho
He learned how to live like he meant it
Going at life like a race in a full dead heat
He sang like he knew every story

Daddy had a pocket of songs
That would charm the Northwest
A voice out of heaven
That would make sure he'd succeed
        He said work like a dog
        And live like some kind of royalty
        Smile like you mean it
        And don't give away the plot
        Do what you can to be a better neighbor
            Tell 'em the truth
            And show 'em what you've got

Out of little boxes came his
Hand-painted porcelain eyes
He could seem to be sighted
You wouldn't know he was blind
No cane no dog

His radar led him around the world
On that dirt-poor farm
By the time he was grown
He could travel to Denver
He could travel to Prague
He made a good life
And like Jackson he was famous
A rodeo rider and a singer from Idaho
    He said work like a dog
    And live like some kind of royalty
    Smile like you mean it
    And don't give away the plot
    Do what you can to be a better neighbor
        Tell 'em the truth
        And show 'em what you've got

And Halley's flew through the heavens then
And birds began to sing
The light from the comet he couldn't see
Bore down on the town of Nezperce
My father was born in the April dawn
With a spirit full of verse
He was an English-Irish boy
And not a native son
But in that town of small renown
His American heart was won
I'm sure it was the Nez Perce tribe
With their beauty and brilliant shine
Their dancing and their beadwork
And their history in time
Maybe it was the comet itself
Said to be an omen
That drove my father all his life
And made him into a showman
A reader even of Twain himself

Who died in the comet's light
My father had the musical gift
To make up for his loss of sight
Until he was four he could see the things
That would stay with him forever
The little red wagon
The purple violets
The sunny and rainy weather
Destined to be the father of six
(One we never knew)
(One of my siblings referred to her
As a lost mourning dove)
Dad rode the rails to Chicago
And did all the things he meant to
He flirted and conquered and mesmerized
His painted glass eyes sky-blue
Halley returned in '86
And I saw her flying through
The comet's tail seemed as long as time
And my father's story grew
Halley now lives in the Kuiper Belt
Till it's time to come back true
Maybe my father's out there too
And maybe he can see
What I'm hoping is that he can
And that one day he'll see me
In the comet's company
A miracle may come true
I think he's somewhere out there
Where the sky and his eyes are blue
I seem to see him once a day
As I make my way through the world
His powerful voice I still can hear
When my own bright flag is furled

He said work like a dog
And live like some kind of royalty
Smile like you mean it
And don't give away the plot
Do what you can to be a better neighbor
    Tell 'em the truth
    And show 'em what you've got

95.   Northwest

Little town
In the great Northwest
Wooden tables in the Bread Peddler
Homemade beef stew
And the split pea soup
They are out of today
Coffee of memory
In the hand-thrown cups
The rainy streets on the cloudy afternoon
You and I met in one of these towns
You were living on borrowed time
In Oregon
Eyes so blue
Saw what I saw

No words needed in the rain
You were writing your novel
Every afternoon in this little
Hand-carved town
Like the cafés in France
In the fifties
In Colorado towns in the sixties that I remember
Whispered secrets
Handwritten stories
Quiet afternoons
Writing, just writing
For years
For centuries
While the carriages turned to Buicks
And the kinds of wars we understood
Were over and the parade streets
Swept clean of the ticker tape
Ferns in the windows
        Joni Mitchell on the radio

A rose in a solitary vase bending her head over the last hours of
her beauty
The rain stopped
My writing hand falters
          Goodbye my beloved brother
The novel you were writing
Covered in smoke
Your borrowed time over
Your ashes still unscattered
On the Snake
In the mountains
In the little towns
As you requested
And as we will do
In our borrowed time
In Estes Park
          Before we have run out of time
On the rivers
In the mountains
And in the little towns

20.   You

I've thought about you all day now
Off in the wide Northwest
With its pine trees and memories
Where the Snake River
Plunges through the hills
Where Chief Joseph
Found no sweet relief
Where buffalo roamed
And our lives were young
And innocent
Before our fires burned the world away

You are the river and the tall pines
You are all the thunder and the gold of the sun
You are the silence
You are the moon
You are the men who could walk it
Through forests of piñon and pine

I sang tonight and thought about your face
Your eyes were in the room where I stood still
I saw you where you work and rest and smile
Sing and play and dance your beauty without knowing
You are beautiful—you don't know it
Which makes you that more beautiful
The cities rise between us their towers and their stones
Full of longing for something on the western plains that
Beckons, breathes, holds
The hoofs of horses while the wind
Pushes through the manes on ponies of the plains
Stark with beauty like you
They have no idea they are beautiful
Where the great Rocky Mountains rise I would walk the
Lakes and the shadowed trails where
Columbine and paintbrush

Blossom with you
You who are the blossom
You who are earth
You who are song
You who are the smile that was lost
The youth I have regained
The sorrow I could never feel
The love I thought I had found
You are the river and the tall pines
You are all the thunder and the gold of the sun
You are the silence
You are the moon
The stars
And the beginning
Of everything that is right in the world

97. Narrow-Gage

Hear that whistle blowing
Down the long tracks
Think of all the times we
Rode those cars
San Francisco to New York
In summertime
Winter rain and comfort
In the bars
I can hear the singing of the aspen
Colorado through the pass
Narrow-gages—memories of gold mines
When the West was young
And sweet and prime
Long before the buffalo were slaughtered
Long before I met you on the path
Long after our destiny was dreaming
Loving through the falling tears and wrath
Living in the times before the fever
We were taken slowly by surprise
Listen to the singing of the pine trees
Looking deep into your sweet blue eyes
If I hear that song before the sunset
Near enough but never in my reach
I will follow in my heart forever
To the place of diamonds on the beach
So the past runs through my dream like rivers
Pulling back the shadows from my eyes
I can see the future from my present
I can face the past without disguise

98.   The Ballad of Jackson Sundown—

Born in Nezperce, Idaho
An American legend son
He grew up
When the buffalo were running
Chief Joseph was his uncle
He rode ponies from the start
He had a way with horses
They understood he had a heart

He fought in the Nez Perce War
With his uncles and his kin
The slaughter and the blood
And bluecoats winning
They chased him and his family
A thousand miles or more
Till half were dead and
Half would count the score

When the war was over
He was fourteen, still alive
He fled north to Canada
With Sitting Bull he'd strive
By eighteen eighty-five
He had learned his deepest pride
All the horses he would tame
All of them he'd ride

All the Nez Perce Appaloosas
All the many grays
All the brilliant runners
All the stripped-down bays
In the Pendleton rodeo
Every year he'd win a prize
Soon he was the golden boy
He was brilliant in all eyes

Rodeos from western states
Wanted him to ride
He traveled like a king and had
The pick and had the pride
His fame, it would precede him
Most cowboys then were white
The crowds were all enormous
When Jackson had the night

Jackson dressed in buckskin
Wore his chaps and all his beads
A scarf tied to his forehead
Broke those broncos with their speed
Some rode against the Nez Perce
But soon Jackson was the king
His competition seldom rode
When he was in the ring
They bowed
Against the famous eagle's wing

Jackson in his forties
Finally found himself a wife
Riding fewer rodeos
Getting older had its price
At fifty-two he rode the broncos
In the Pendleton again
He came in second place
And said he'd never ride again

The rodeos were over
And those years of riding horse
Had wrecked his body
He would have to find some other source
He was keeping to his promise
When a sculptor found him home

Proctor asked Sundown to sit
Wanted him and him alone

Soon as they were started
The artist wanted every pose
Jackson's face, his hands
His feet, his head, his eyes, his nose
They worked for many months
And finally the sculptor said, "My friend,
I've got to see your body,
See you ride those broncs again"

Jackson didn't want to do it
He was nearing fifty-three
But the sculptor said, "A year's expenses,
And what's more, I'll pay your fee"
He'd foot the bills for Jackson's life
Win or lose, it didn't matter
It would just be his delight
Just to see the other cowboys scatter

And watch that wondrous body
Arch the neck of some great brute
See the flanks and see the flesh
As they plunged out of the chute
So it was 1916 Jackson rode
He was truly in his prime
It would be Pendleton again
At the greatest rodeo of all that time

The other cowboys shivered at those
Hand-carved leather boots
Jackson showed up cool as ice
In his best summer suit
Black hair braided down his back

Tied with a leather thong
Gloves of Native tooling
While he hummed a Nez Perce song

His handsome face was peaceful
The tribal prayers were prayed
He'd do his best, he told them all
And said the gods were with him
Angel was his bronco
A horse with famous tricks
While Sundown flapped his hat
The horse was pulling jumps and kicks

So wild were Angel's antics
That people screamed and shouted
Nothing like it, not before or since
There wasn't any doubt
That Jackson won that day
On Angel as she whirled
The highest prize they ever gave
The championship of the world

Hands down in one great ride
A hundred years to the day
Pendleton wove their pride
Into a grand display
Jackson up on Angel's back
His hat up in the air
The Nez Perce in his prime
He sent up his own prayer

For Sitting Bull and Crazy Horse
Chief Joseph and the rest
His cousins and his Nez Perce tribe
He held them to his breast

A prayer for all the Nez Perce
Who weathered every storm
Who fought the bluecoats to the end
Whose lives were cut and torn

From Georgia to Montana
From the White Bird pass to Canada
The Trail of Tears has never ended
And it never will
Goodbye to all the buffalo
And all the bluecoats too
In history they ride off in
A story old and new

So here's to Jackson Sundown
And the last time that he rode
That brought him into history
Which time cannot erode
May Nez Perce dreams remind us all
Of the bravery of man
The beauty of his spirit
The courage of his clan
Celebrating Jackson Sundown
Where buffalo ghosts still roam
And now he lives in history
The West is still his home

99.   Ravi

That day we went to hear Ravi play
In the Riverside cathedral
I must have drunk from the fairies' brew
And felt a sense primeval

When Ravi's fingers stroked the strings
My heart began to sing
As if I knew the music from
So far beyond the sting
Of lovers' kisses
Mother's twist

The blowing horns the
Pounding fist
Relieved of rhyme and reason
Plunged into an ancient season

For days the sitar
Roamed my blood
I could see nothing as it stood
But walked along the river's edge
Beholding eyes behind the hood

And thought myself beyond the touch
Reality was gone so much
For days I walked on air and cloud
The little things of life were loud

The bleating horns, the singing birds
Were nothing to the music heard
Beyond the city, past all times
I sought for pillows drenched in
Rhymes

One day it passed
This strange event
When I was on my dinner bent
It rushed off to some other soul
Whose time was spent in discontent

And settled there to give repent
From present worries, time unspent
And they were suddenly released
Their painful thoughts
There and then ceased

Even for a little while they had
To laugh, they had to smile
To think that there was nothing good
In worrying about the world

100. Croz

A bright and flashing light
flying through the night
of stars and old guitars
bound for Earth and Mars
He was out of sight
He knew how to fight
knew how to write
lived with all his might
each and every night
Knew that he was right
sparked our delight
He was like a kite
in skies of broken light
He was like a king
ruling on the wing
fighting everything
God,
and how he could sing

101.   Roses

The roses on the stage
The reddest shade of blood
The concert master with his
Smile reveals the night
With light and dancing stars
Begins the magic flood
I step out on the stage
And find the melody
My voice goes up

And with it all my sorrows flee
For I have no illusions when I sing
Only when the echoes
Of the encores fade
I feel the roses lose their color
In the shade
My steps proceed me to the
Wings of memory
                And you, the only you
                There ever was, retreat
                The roses weep to see you
                As you disappear

102.   Never Die

He was glancing at my ankles
Then he stared
For it was summer
And my legs were tanned and bared
His eyes moved up to mine and then we smiled
For many years to come my dreams were wild
We only spoke across two oceans' span
He said come when you will, come when you can
Love is never easy I would say
Never what it seems from night to day
He was the view I longed so much to see
Whenever I felt beautiful and free
And sometimes now I wish I could just cry
For he is gone who said he'd never die

103.   War

All the stars were burning
And he could not stop the war
The shells were bursting 'round him
And he knew what they were for
Murdering the innocent and
Shoring up the ditch
His helmet flew across the dust
His gun was in the midst
Now I see it—all he saw
But what good can that stay
War is hell, they told me then
It's everything, they say
They brought it down upon us
To carry us away
Surprising us with beauty
At the dawning of the day
Behind the clouds the sun was bright
I could hear my heart
I'm not a soldier, I kept saying
I could live apart
I could live in poverty
I could live in sin
I could live in infamy
My life could begin
I could drink the wine of pleasure
I could see the stars
If I make it out of this
I could fly to Mars
Soldiers are the muscle
Of the nightmares of the kings
Though they may not wear the crowns
The coronets or rings
They can bring their force
Upon the gentle of the land
Push them down into the mud

until they cannot stand
How would kings survive
Without the wars that they provoke
Most of them would see their worlds
And treasures up in smoke
If we keep protecting those
Who want to rule the world
When will we be living free
When will our banners be unfurled

104.   For Pia

I love this old, cracked basin
Like a spiderweb in ice
A jar of French perfume upon the rim
Hand towels stitched with scenes of childhood
Faded by time and years
And in the living room my old friend
Radiant past her tears
What has time not done to us
Through the passing light
Bringing vibrant memories that
Sail us through the night
We talk of children and of death
And of the silent air
Outside the windows trees are bending
Leaves without a care
Summers wandering through our dreams
Our talk is quick and spare
The silences between our words draw
Pictures rich and rare
The quiet city breathes, remembering
Days of all our glory
The triumphs and the victories
The incandescent story
Ever new
My friend, we love the view
Just me and you
You are my own

105. Amen

I am here for the long dance and the high lights
I'll take another shot at the moon
I'll play this hand over and over
Till the rain comes down the monsoon
I'm here for the trials of the century
I'm here for the face in the crowd
I will sing about heroes and monsters
We have plenty, for both are allowed
Like Dante and Virgil and Jesus
There's room for everyone here
So pass me my pen and my whiskey
While I write of your joy and my fear
Come over beside the window
We can see the stars from here
Falling from heaven and Mercury
Past comets fly through our sphere
There's nothing to be afraid of
We've been here time and again
Bound through space on our blue Earth
The nightingale, thrush, and the wren
Murmurations painting the twilight
With promises we try to keep
With rhymes our words insisting
As we meander toward the biggest sleep
      Amen Amen Amen

Acknowledgments

I am indebted to my husband, Louis Nelson, for our lives together. In 2016, Louis challenged me to write 365 poems—one each day. Many of these poems make up *Sometimes It's Heaven*.

To Katherine DePaul, who keeps the fires burning.

To Susan Raihofer, who sees the light.

To Russ Walden for listening.

Gratitude to my father, Chuck; my mother, Marjorie; my siblings David, Michael, Denver, and Holly; and to my granddaughter, Hollis. You have all inspired me to write, to sing, to live, to breathe—to celebrate with joy and gratitude. You have brought all the poetry in my world to life.

And always to my son, Clark Collin Taylor.
1959–1992
RIP

Thank you.

About the Author

Written with the bold vulnerability that Judy Collins is best known for, *Sometimes It's Heaven* is a timeless collection of poetry that reaches audiences right where they are.

Throughout her six-decade long career, Judy Collins has inspired audiences with sublime vocals, boldly vulnerable songwriting, personal life triumphs, and a firm commitment to social activism. In the 1960s, she evoked both the idealism and steely determination of a generation united against social and environmental injustices. Six decades later, her luminescent presence shines brightly as new generations bask in the glow of her iconic fifty-five-album body of work, and heed inspiration from her spiritual discipline to thrive in the music industry for half a century.

The award-winning singer-songwriter is esteemed for her imaginative interpretations of traditional and contemporary folk standards and her own poetically poignant original compositions. Her stunning rendition of Joni Mitchell's "Both Sides Now" from her landmark 1967 album, *Wildflowers*, has been entered into the Grammy Hall of Fame. Judy's dreamy and sweetly intimate version of "Send in the Clowns," a ballad written by Stephen Sondheim for the Broadway musical *A Little Night Music*, won Song of the Year at the 1975 Grammy Awards. She's garnered several top-ten hits and gold- and platinum-selling albums. In 2008, contemporary and classic artists such as Rufus Wainwright, Shawn Colvin, Dolly Parton, Joan Baez, and Leonard Cohen honored her legacy with the album *Born to the Breed: A Tribute to Judy Collins*.

Judy began her impressive music career at thirteen as a piano prodigy dazzling audiences performing Mozart's *Concerto for Two Pianos*, but the hard-luck tales and rugged sensitivity of folk revival music by artists such as Woody Guthrie and Pete Seeger seduced her away from a life as a concert pianist. Her path pointed to a lifelong love affair with the guitar and pursuit of emotional truth in lyrics. The focus and regimented practice of classical music, however, would be a source of strength to her inner core as she navigated the highs and lows of the music business.

In 1961, she released her masterful debut, *A Maid of Constant Sorrow*, which featured interpretative works of social poets of the time such as Bob Dylan, Phil Ochs, and Tom Paxton. This began a wonderfully fertile thirty-five-year creative relationship with Jac Holzman and Elektra Records. Around this time Judy became a tastemaker within the thriving Greenwich Village folk community and brought other singer-songwriters to a wider audience, including poet/musician Leonard Cohen, and musicians Joni Mitchell and Randy Newman. Throughout the 60s, 70s, 80s, 90s, and up to the present, she has remained a vital artist, enriching her catalog with critically acclaimed albums while balancing a robust touring schedule.

The cultural treasure's 55th album, *Spellbound*, was released in February 2022, and finds Judy enjoying an artistic renaissance. The thirteen-song album is a special entry in her oeuvre. It marks the first time ever she wrote all the songs on one of her albums. It features twelve new recently written modern folk songs, and a bonus track of her evergreen "The Blizzard." *Spellbound* is an introspective and impressionistic album. It unfolds as if Judy curated a museum exhibit of her life, and welcomed us into a retrospective of her most formative moments, some big and public, and some intensely personal and intimate. *Spellbound* was nominated in the Best Folk Album category at the 65th Recording Academy Grammy Awards in 2023.

Judy has also authored several books, including the powerful and inspiring *Sanity & Grace* and her extraordinary memoir, *Sweet Judy Blue Eyes: My Life in Music*. In *Cravings*, she provides a no-holds-barred account of her harrowing struggle with compulsive overeating, and the journey that led her to a solution. Alternating between chapters on her life and those of the many diet gurus she has encountered along the way (Atkins, Jean Nidetch of Weight Watchers, and Andrew Weil, to name a few), *Cravings* is the culmination of Judy's genuine desire to share what she's learned so that no one has to follow her heartrending path to recovery.

Sometimes It's Heaven

Judy Collins is as creatively vigorous as ever, writing, touring worldwide, and nurturing fresh talent. She is a modern-day Renaissance woman who is a filmmaker, record label head, musical mentor, and an in-demand keynote speaker for mental health and suicide prevention. She continues to create music of hope and healing that lights up the world and speaks to the heart.

Andrews McMeel Publishing
a division of Andrews McMeel Universal
1130 Walnut Street, Kansas City, Missouri 64106

www.andrewsmcmeel.com

25 26 27 28 29 KPR 10 9 8 7 6 5 4 3 2 1

ISBN: 978-1-5248-9436-8

Library of Congress Control Number: 2024944567

Editor: Patty Rice
Art Director/Designer: Diane Marsh
Production Editor: David Shaw
Production Manager: Shona Burns

On the cover: Judy Collins, age thirteen, after performing a
Mozart Concerto K365 with the Antonia Brico Symphony
Orchestra, Phipps Auditorium, in Denver, Colorado's City
Park, February 1953. From Judy Collins's personal collection.

ATTENTION: SCHOOLS AND BUSINESSES
Andrews McMeel books are available at quantity
discounts with bulk purchase for educational, business, or
sales promotional use. For information, please email the
Andrews McMeel Publishing Special Sales Department:
sales@andrewsmcmeel.com.